Wildlife in church
and churchyard

Wildlife in church and churchyard

Plants, animals and their management

Nigel Cooper

2nd edition

Church House Publishing
Church House,
Great Smith Street,
London
SW1P 3NZ

ISBN 0 7151 7587 4 2nd edition
(ISBN 0 7151 7574 2 1st edition)

First published 1995
Second edition 2001

Published 2001 for the Council
for the Care of Churches of the
Church of England by Church
House Publishing.

First edition copyright © Central
Board of Finance of the Church
of England 1995
Second edition copyright © The
Archbishops' Council 1995, 2001

Cover design by Visible Edge

Typeset in 9pt Sabon

Printed in England by
Latimer Trend and Co. Ltd,
Plymouth

Contents

List of illustrations

Preface

Churchyards happily bring together my work as a priest in the Church of England with my interest in biology and concern for conservation. It has been my pleasure to have been involved with churchyard conservation since 1986 and my privilege to have served on my Diocesan Advisory Committee since 1991. In that time I have learned a great deal, mainly from others with much more experience.

This booklet is designed to expand the advice on the management of wildlife given in chapter 10 of the fourth edition of *The Churchyards Handbook*. I hope it will prove a useful store of advice for people in parishes actually caring for churchyards. Such people may find it valuable to seek additional help from others such as nature conservationists and Diocesan Advisory Committees. Local authorities and other groups responsible for maintaining church-yards and cemeteries should also find the booklet helpful.

Throughout I have spoken of 'churchyards', as this is a Church of England publication. Nearly all that I have written could apply equally to the curtilage of all places of worship and to all burial grounds. I hope that local authority officers and people of other denominations will substitute their appropriate terminology when reading this booklet.

I am very aware of how much my own thinking has changed over the years and I am certain that what is considered good practice now will change in the future. This revised edition will itself need revising in time; there has only been opportunity for very minor revisions in most chapters (excepting trees and landscape design). The more people try to implement the advice in this edition, the sooner we shall realize what does need changing. My advice is tentative and not applicable to all circumstances, but this approach may not be evident from the text, where I have generally been dogmatic in my style for clarity. This sort of publication is inevitably full of 'oughts' and 'shoulds'. I do not want those words to condemn, deflate or depress people: I would rather people caught a sense of wonder from the life of the churchyard to inspire them.

Acknowledgements

I have learned so much from so many people. I particularly want to thank those who are named below who have read and commented on parts or all of the text in the course of its production. They are: David Andrews, Helen Clothier, Melvyne Crow, John Dobson, John Hunter, Tony Hutson, Hugh Johnson, David Lodge, Theresa Orpin, Marya Parker, Oliver Rackham, Nick Radford, Eric Robinson, Tim Ruggles-Brise, Gillie Sargent, John Shead, Peter Spencer, Ernest Stroud, Barry Thompson and Stephen Westover.

My friends and colleagues who have worked with me in the Essex Churchyards Conservation Group deserve special mention. They are: Ken Adams, David Bain, Lynda Cheney, Graham Feldwick, Dorothy Hancock, Chris Manning-Press, Chris Miles, Doug Shipman and Meg Watson.

I want to thank Eve Dennis, who was the Director of the Church and Conservation Project and its offshoot, the Living Churchyard Project. Her knowledge, her help and her encouragement have been invaluable. She has read all the text, as have Thomas Cocke, Ghillean Prance and Max Walters. I am very grateful for their most helpful suggestions. The errors that remain are evidence of my wilfulness!

I also wish to thank the Chelmsford Diocesan Advisory Committee for permission to use the text of their official advice on trees which I wrote with much help from other members.

Finally I thank my area bishop for his encouragement, and my parish and family for their generous tolerance of my enthusiasm for churchyards.

For this second edition I would like to thank David Bain and Lin Wenlock (both of the Essex Churchyards Conservation Group) for their comments and Miss Shelia Cameron QC, Chancellor of the Diocese of Chelmsford, for permission to use material from her *Guidance on Trees*.

Abbreviations

Code s   Paragraph section of *Care of Churches and*
                 Ecclesiastical Jurisdiction Measure: Code of
                 Practice, Church House Publishing, 1993

Handbook p   Page number in *The Churchyards Handbook*,
                 fourth edition, edited by Thomas Cocke for the
                 Council for the Care of Churches, Church House
                 Publishing, 2001

D1, etc.   Suggested action points for dioceses

P1, etc.   Suggested action points for parishes

chapter 1
Caring for creation

The churchyard is a sermon not only in stones but in plants and animals. Like the changes in fashion that have affected the building, there have been changes in the way churchyards have been cared for. These have come about as different understandings of God's nature have developed. We are currently going through a phase of major change, principally in our understanding of God's relationship to the creation, and this booklet has been written in response to this.

The opening chapter of Genesis proclaims on God's authority that the creation is good and yet people have felt it also to be the realm of suffering and evil. Some have believed that as the image-bearers of God it has been the duty of people to train and to subdue these evil forces in the non-human, natural world. But as fears grow for the environment, we are beginning to wonder if the greatest force for evil may actually lie within ourselves.

The science of ecology helps us appreciate the interdependence of all life on this planet. We can no longer believe that our relationship to the natural world is a simple hierarchy: God's will being imposed upon the brute creation through human agency and the brute creation serving God through meeting human needs. There must be a mutuality; the natural world sustains our life while we must nurture it.

Churchyards offer places where we can catch this vision and act upon it. They can be places where we can practise living harmoniously with our fellow creatures, treasuring their presence among us. They can speak of how we see God's presence in creation and how we believe God wishes us to care for that creation. They can aim to be places where the human needs of those who use the churchyard and value its historic treasures, and the needs of plants and animals for a home, are in balance.

There are many people within the Church, and many more without, who are looking for a new attitude to the world in its fragility and for a congruent lifestyle. It is a common accusation that the Church and Christian theology have promoted a grasping and careless attitude to the natural world. Whatever the truth of this accusation about the past, and there is both justice and injustice in it, the Church today can be at the forefront of moves towards treasuring the creation. This will help those looking to the Church for a lead and it might help the Church to restore its credibility amongst those with a concern for the environment. Nature conservation in church-yards is important not just because they are valuable sanctuaries for wildlife, but also because they can set an example within local com-munities of how to live in greater harmony with all creation.

As Christians we believe that the non-human world has value because it is valued by God, its creator. God, indeed, delights in it. If this is so, plants and animals and the whole environment have a value independent of their usefulness or convenience for us, and this in turn implies that they deserve our care. In this view, managing the churchyard becomes not only a ministry to the human users but also a ministry to the creatures living there.

fig. 1
Stonecrop
flowering on
a grave.

chapter 2

How to manage the churchyard

Importance of churchyard conservation

'The last two decades of the twentieth century saw a gathering revolution in popular attitudes towards nature conservation, and the churchyard has come into focus as one of our most important national assets in terms of the habitat it provides for a wide range of grasses, mosses, lichens, ferns, fungi, flowers, trees (both native and introduced), insects, reptiles, birds and mammals.' (*Handbook*, p. 95)

Since the mid-1980s the recognition of the importance of churchyards for nature conservation has grown and much more experience has been gained.

There is a growing awareness of the value of churchyards as both representative habitats and as refuges for threatened species. The most important habitat in churchyards is the grassland. Agricultural examples of unimproved grassland, popularly thought of as flowery meadows, are being rapidly lost to intensive farming methods. The stonework is also very significant, especially in the south of England where so little rock is naturally exposed. Veteran trees, we now realize, provide homes for many rare insects and plants; such trees are common in churchyards. Churchyards are also important because they form a patchwork of sites making it more likely that threatened species may be able to disperse from one site to another. Because they have a high social profile, churchyards are also important in educating the public about conservation.

A number of plant species, even those that are not exceptionally rare, are highly dependent on churchyards for their long-term survival. In Norfolk, for example,[1] it has been estimated that about 50 per cent of the county populations of pignut, lady's bedstraw, sorrel, burnet saxifrage, ox-eye daisy and cowslip are to be found in churchyards. Similarly with other groups of plants and animals, from lichens, through insects, to bats, churchyards provide a base for significant populations of threatened species.

Planning protection

A few churchyards have been legally designated Sites of Special Scientific Interest (SSSIs) and some churchyards have become nature reserves. These will have a very professional management plan. It is more common for a churchyard to be designated a 'Site of Importance for Nature Conservation' (SINC) or equivalent, for example ten per cent of Suffolk churchyards are so designated. In these cases it will be up to the church to draw up the management plan, though help should be available. These designated sites do need special care.

SITES OF IMPORTANCE FOR NATURE CONSERVATION (SINCs)

- SINC is one of many terms for these locally designated sites; others include Site of Biological Importance, County Wildlife/Heritage Site, Site of Scientific Interest.

- The administration of the designation of schemes also varies, but generally it is a partnership of English Nature, the local wildlife trust and the planning authority. The conservation agency selects the sites and the planning authority gives a degree of protection to the sites as it chooses.

- The criteria used in selecting sites for designation (in some sort of order of importance for churchyards) are: diversity of species, presence of important populations of rare species, the presence of indicators of continuity, diversity of structure and habitats, contiguity to other wildlife sites, geological interest, existence of historical data and records, situation in an area lacking natural habitats.

- Most churchyards will not score highly on the size criterion but will score on accessibility to the public and educational value. They also usually contain a habitat type that is scarce, that is grassland. The aesthetic appeal of churchyards is also generally high. There is a case for saying that all churchyards with ancient grassland should be designated as SINCs. Their fairly even distribution throughout the landscape makes them more important collectively than their individual size might indicate.

- Parishes should be notified that their churchyard has been designated a SINC and also the diocese (or other denominational body). A list of designated sites should be held by both the diocesan registry and the Diocesan Advisory Committee.

Suggestions for action

D1   Dioceses should draw up a policy for protecting churchyards designated as SINCs, for example 'Activities will not normally be permitted which may destroy or adversely affect, directly or indirectly, a Site of Importance for Nature Conservation.'

D2   Diocesan Advisory Committees should give proper weight to the conservation of the natural heritage alongside other considerations when giving advice to churches.

The wording of the constitution of Diocesan Advisory Committees gives them a role in advising on the use and care of churchyards and burial grounds, in encouraging the appreciation of such places and in publicising methods of conservation. The Code of Practice (s109) states that this 'is clearly wide enough to cover the wildlife aspects'. For many this will be a relatively new field and a body of expertise and information will need to be established. Diocesan Advisory Committees should develop and maintain records on wildlife in the churches and churchyards of the diocese. They will need to build links with local wildlife conservation bodies and with English Nature as the statutory body. These bodies should also be sent the agenda and minutes of Diocesan Advisory Committee meetings if requested, as is recommended for amenity societies (Code s119).

D3   Ecologists should be appointed to Diocesan Advisory Committees.

The constitution of Diocesan Advisory Committees specifies that they should have as members people specializing in different fields. Unfortunately the field of biology is not specified, but with more and more ecological and aboricultural issues coming before Diocesan Advisory Committees, all dioceses would be wise to follow the lead given by some of them in appointing an ecologist to the Diocesan Advisory Committee. The Code of Practice encourages the appointment of specialists in wildlife and trees (Code s87).

In considering applications for certificates, Diocesan Advisory Committees will need to consider whether the proposals threaten wildlife or might contravene national conservation legislation. Parishes (and diocesan chancellors) need advice on how best to protect wildlife along with developing the work of the church and protecting its buildings.

The Diocesan Advisory Committee may recommend that a faculty is only granted with special conditions. These might be that the wildlife is safeguarded in particular ways, or that there is prior evaluation, or that prior recording is undertaken and the records appropriately stored (Code s185).

ACTIVITIES THAT MAY ENDANGER WILDLIFE

- Tree felling and surgery may endanger the tree and associated plants and animals, including bats.
- Church extensions, car parks, ground lowering and trenches may destroy valuable grassland: survey first.
- Repair of walls and paths may eliminate plant cover or entomb bats.
- Moving or repairing monuments may damage lichens and other plants.
- Redundancy: the new holders should be alerted to the wildlife value of the site and its past history of management.
- Minor works, including planting a tree, clearing a path, changing the time of mowing, rehanging a door can all have a major impact on living creatures. They may even be illegal if they affect a protected species.

Managing for conservation

'It is important that the churchyard is managed in a way that helps to preserve and enhance its character as a wildlife habitat, not only in the interests of the parish but also of the wider community, and the parish's churchyard management plan should take this into account.' (Code s79)

The management plan is part of a four-step process. The first step is to survey the churchyard for its current wildlife so it is known what is to be conserved and what may be developed. Secondly a management plan can be drawn up and put into practice. Not everyone can be consulted before the plan is adopted but it is very important at least to explain what is going on in the churchyard to those who may visit it, and this is the third step. Finally the plan must be reviewed periodically. The Fourth Edition of *The Churchyards Handbook* puts the management plan into the context of a seven step procedure (pp. 94–101).

Step one: the survey

P1   Arrange for a competent survey to be made of the wildlife in the church and churchyard.

If conservation of wildlife is to be taken seriously, it is essential to survey the churchyard to discover what is already growing and living there. All parishes should be encouraged to seek a professional survey of their churchyard, as surprising rarities can be found in unexpected places. Professional surveys, which may need to be paid for (Code s127), should be undertaken when there is a possible threat to the natural heritage.

At other times parishes may attempt their own survey without more expert help. In the first instance they can ask someone with an interest in wildflowers to look over the churchyard through the year to make a note of which plants flower, and when. This will give a basic guide and may reveal a surprising range of species. The parish may also need expert help.

The availability of people to survey a churchyard and give management advice will vary from place to place. The local wildlife trust will often be able to help.

The extent of the survey will depend on the level of expertise of the surveyor and the time available. The survey will need to cover the grassland in some detail and a review of the other habitats present. Some groups such as bryophytes (mosses and liverworts), lichens, and invertebrates (insects, etc.) require specialists to undertake their survey. Specialist surveyors should be asked to survey any churchyard that is under particular threat, e.g. a survey of lichens is needed if headstone removal is proposed.

A basic survey would include a sketch map of the churchyard, which should have marked on it the different areas of grass and also other wildlife features, e.g. walls and compost heaps. For each grass area there should be a list of the flowering plants seen over the year. Most people have difficulty identifying plants in their vegetative state and so it is essential that a few small trial areas are left uncut for a season to give all the plants a chance to flower and so be identified. The current and past patterns of managing the churchyard should also be recorded and some photographs taken.

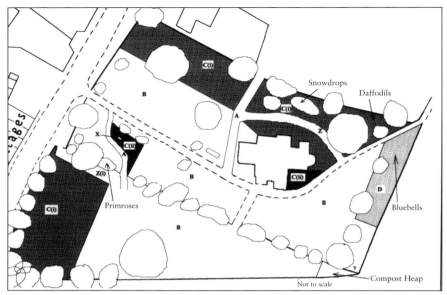

fig. 2   An example of a straightforward management plan.

Acknowledgements: Great Maplestead PCC; Map © Crown Copyright

A	Grass paths	X	Memorial (See report)
B	Regularly cut grassland	Y	Hay pile
C (i)	Spring meadowland	Z	New grass path
C (ii)	Summer meadowland	Z (i)	New grass path (Agreed
D	Grassland cut in rotation		since date of report)

See report to St Giles
Great Maplestead PCC
"Churchyard Survey" for a
full explanation of this plan.

Key to fig. 2

The surveyor should meet the people involved in looking after the churchyard at least once, and on the last visit go round the churchyard discussing possible management ideas with representatives of the parish. The management ideas brought up in this discussion should be recorded by the surveyor and attached to the survey.

A copy of the survey report should be left with the parish where it should be kept safely with other parochial records and documents. Another copy should be deposited in an appropriate local record centre for wildlife. All the surveys for one area should be kept together.

Step two: the management plan

P2   Draw up a management plan for the churchyard based on the survey and then try to follow it.

The survey is one of the starting points for working out a management plan. Such a plan is a key tool for the parish in looking after a churchyard, as is recommended by the Code of Practice (s75).

A management plan provides a framework for maintenance and management which – while observing the churchyard's primary function as a resting place for the dead – will respect and encourage the diversity of wildlife, in a place where it is entirely appropriate for it to seek sanctuary. The local managers, perhaps with advice from a naturalist, must discuss what is the best strategy for their particular churchyard. The 'best' in this context may seem a compromise to the naturalist, but there are many other factors to be considered in the care of a churchyard in addition to wildlife.

Chief among these other considerations are local opinion, historic heritage and practical possibilities. Those managing a churchyard may or may not be really keen to encourage wildlife, but they will face much criticism if they do not show they are listening to local opinion. It is usually a matter of proceeding in small stages with much education and public relations work along the way. Those concerned with the church building, certain monuments and the general fabric will need to be assured that the historic and human treasures of the site will not be jeopardized by the promotion of wildlife conservation. Above all, the money and person-power available to do the management work may be very limited, uncertain or unreliable. Management plans must not be too ambitious or unrealistic.

The written plan needs to be as helpful as possible. Often the best way is to provide an annotated map showing, for example, the areas to be cut at which times of the year, or important stretches of wall for wildlife. At the bottom of the map a few comments could be made that do not fit easily on the map itself, such as avoiding the use of chemical treatments throughout the churchyard. The personal contacts established by the surveyor will be as important as any document in changing the outlook and enthusiasm of the churchyard managers.

Step three: explaining the management plan

P3   Explain the management plan as widely as possible.

If the management ideas set out in the plan are to be followed in future years, they must come to receive local support, and good communication of the ideas involved will achieve this. If the value of churchyards for conservation is two-fold, not just preserving wildlife but also giving a lead to others, there is an added reason for explaining what is going on.

Once a parish has adopted a management plan, it must indicate what it is doing. At the very least it must put up a poster on the noticeboard or in the porch: many churchyard advisers have specially produced ones they can issue to parishes. It is very useful also to display the management plan, particularly the sketch map. It is not enough to put a notice in front of some long grass saying 'conservation area': the whole churchyard should be managed with wildlife in mind.

Interpreting what people can see is essential if they are to understand wildlife in churchyards and appreciate it. Some churches have an extensive display with photographs of plants or animals found in the churchyard. Others keep a list of the plants currently in flower or birds nesting, whilst others may think it appropriate to put a small label next to some particular feature. If the churchyard has entered a competition or, better still, won a prize, these can be displayed. These displays all need to be temporary affairs, not least so that they don't get out of date and gain that faded-curled-water-marked look that comes over anything left in a church too long. Permanent notices will probably need a faculty.

Parish magazines are an excellent way of explaining not just the initial changes but also reporting how the wildlife is responding. It is a joy when the church guide book contains a section on the churchyard, its monuments, geology and wildlife.

Children can also be involved. All sorts of aspects of the school curriculum can be addressed in a topic on churchyards and many primary schools will find a churchyard within walking distance. Churches and schools are already used to cooperating over visiting a church for religious education and perhaps history. Where the churchyard is at least tolerant of wildlife it proves a valuable educational resource for other subject areas. Parts of national curriculum science and geography, especially subjects such as rocks and weathering, soils, variety of life, fossils, and care for the environment, can be tackled in a churchyard.

The churchyard is equally useful in adult education. Naturalists can be encouraged to visit the churchyard where they can study nature within the wider context of the Christian beliefs about creation. It is a good idea to organize guided walks or open evenings, and a local branch of the Workers' Educational Association might be able to help with these.

Step four: reviewing the plan

P4   Review what is happening in the churchyard and the management plan every few years.

As the management plan is put into effect all sorts of minor and major changes will be made. Sometimes these changes will be due to accidents such as bad weather or stolen equipment. After one season there should be some informal discussion on how the original plans could be improved. This general review of the plan could lead to its formal change.

In addition, there needs to be a review of the impact of the plan on the wildlife. Perhaps after one year some of the major plants could be looked at to see if they have changed significantly in quantity. It would be wise to undertake a thorough survey of the churchyard after five years to monitor the changes that have taken place. This would lead to a review of the management plan to see whether it was having the desired effect or whether new opportunities had arisen. The biology of a churchyard is unpredictable and fluctuates widely from year to year, making this process an art and not a science.

chapter 3
Grassland

Why grassland is important

Of all the different habitats in a churchyard, grassland is the one that probably has the most importance for wildlife conservation. The debate over its management is very contentious.

'With the ploughing up or spraying of old meadowland, many meadow flowers have become very dependent on churchyards for survival. The Nature Conservancy Council estimated in the 1980s that about 98 per cent of herb-rich meadowland had been lost over the previous 30 years. In lowland counties, some meadow flowers have as much as 50 per cent of their surviving population in churchyards.' (*Handbook*, p. 109)

Before the coming of agriculture to Britain there would have been pockets of grassland within the wildwood that covered most of these islands, perhaps even as extensive as a savannah. These grassy glades were mostly maintained by large grazers such as wild ox. As the woods were felled, some of the fields were used for grazing pasture or as hay meadows. The wild plants and animals of the glades then extended their ranges into these fields. Some fields were set aside around churches for burials. These churchyards have largely escaped the changes to intensive agriculture that have eliminated the rich wildlife from so many farms (it is even possible that some of the grass clones are over 1,000 years old). That is why churchyard grassland is so important in nature conservation.

The idea behind the recommendations that follow is the conservation of grassland wildlife balanced with what is possible and acceptable in a churchyard. Grassland management for wildlife is a matter of imitating farming practices.

Management and mowing

P5 Keep up the traditional way of looking after your particular churchyard unless there are good reasons for change.

The primary concern of conservation is always to care for what is already there. The plants and animals living in a churchyard will be suited to whatever management they are consistently receiving and might well decline or disappear if it is changed in any way. Grassland species are particularly vulnerable to management change. Unlike, for example, a woodland, the appearance and nature of a grassland can change in only two or three years if grass cutting ceases or if regular mowing commences. This could be long enough to cause the extinction at that site of species that had been common only three years before. Once extinct, even if suitable conditions are re-established, it may be a very long time before the old species return, if ever, depending on how close the nearest remaining populations are for migrants to come from or whether there is still a viable seed bank in the soil.

fig. 3
Grass rich in flowers.

Continuity of management does not mean keeping to a rigid timetable: that was never done in the past. Every few years a combination of unusual weather patterns and human coincidences would have meant abnormal management. These interruptions of the normal regime probably allow some species to continue at the site because it is only in these unusual conditions that they can propagate themselves. We know very little about the role of these little catastrophes, but some plant species, for example, may usually need short grass to avoid competition from taller growing plants, but also need the occasional year when the grass is not cut to allow them to flower and produce seed.

This is not a plea for churchyards to adopt a short-back-and-sides treatment, but it is a caution against the headlong rush to cease frequent mowing that is gaining popularity in the name of conservation. Where grass has been left long for many years, it should remain so. Where it is short, a very careful study should be made before it is allowed to grow long. If there has been a change in management within the past five or so years, it may be wise to consider returning to the old management system.

P6   Collect the grass cuttings after each mow.

Removing the grass cuttings keeps the soil fertility down, which is of advantage to the more unusual plants. This was probably general practice in the past. Recent studies suggest that there is a decline in species diversity after about ten years after ceasing to remove cuttings.[1] If the cuttings are not just a fine dusting, as will be the case where the grass is mowed regularly, but are clods of mashed grass from rotary mowers or are sheaths of longer grass cut by strimmers, then there is the added and immediate danger of smothering the plants below. In fact, this is so effective at killing plants that it is the best method of clearing vegetation without using chemical herbicides. Fallen leaves in autumn must also be removed and, preferably, composted.

When the grass is short, the cuttings can usually be collected in the grass box attached to the mower. When the grass is long the cuttings have to be removed separately. One difficulty is deciding when to rake up the cuttings. Generally it seems best to leave them lying a few days so that any seeds can drop out and insects can move onto the uncut plants. On the other hand, some insects, particularly brown butterflies in July, may lay their eggs on the cut stems. Where these butterflies are known to be present, the cuttings must be raked up straightaway. If it is impossible to rake up the cuttings at every mow, it is most important to concentrate efforts on removing the summer cut which contains the largest quantity of nutrients. Local people with horses or other animals may be encouraged to take the hay.

Clearly, removing the grass cuttings can prove a good deal of work, especially for those who have already laboured long in cutting the grass. There may not always be the time to achieve the ideal of removing all

ASSESSING SOIL FERTILITY

Soils with low fertility have the highest conservation interest and the widest range of plants. Soils with high fertility will be colonized by tall-growing plants if left uncut.

An estimate of soil fertility can be made by examining the plants already growing on it.

If the grasses have wide leaves (over 7 mm) and the other plants are tall weeds like nettle, thistle, cow parsley and hogweed, then the soil is fertile and the grass is already long or has been left long recently.

If the grasses have leaves between 2 mm and 8 mm wide and the other plants include lawn weeds like white clover, daisy and ribwort plantain, then the soil is fertile but the grass has been regularly mown for a long while.

If the grasses have leaves less than 3 mm wide, or the non-grass plants are not common weeds, or the non-grass plants make up more than 30 per cent of the sward, then the soil is probably infertile and it should be surveyed by someone competent to identify the plants and the community to which they belong.

the cuttings. A compromise is to remove the cuttings at least from areas rich in flowers and/or some of the longer summer cuts.

P7　**Increase the diversity of the types of grass by mowing different areas at different intervals.**

It is obvious that grass cut once a week will look like a lawn, while grass that is cut once a year may look like a hay field. The appearance is very different, and so too are the plant species that will flourish under these two treatments. Insects and other animals may also vary between the two types, but more often flourish best if a variety of grass height is maintained in a churchyard. Many churchyards will already have a range of grass-cutting regimes, but it may benefit the wildlife gradually to change the balance, position and type of these different regimes.

The areas for the different cutting regimes need to be marked on the management map of the churchyard. In choosing particular treatments for different areas many factors have to be considered: what has been the traditional management of the area, what is the soil type and what sort of plants will grow there, what will be aesthetically pleasing and acceptable to churchyard users, how much work can those who care for the churchyard manage?

The following table of different grassland management regimes sets out the main choices.

Basic grassland management regimes

GRASS CUTTING	SUITABLE FOR
Short grass Cut frequently during the growing season, every one to three weeks. Set cutting height at 38 to 50 mm for most areas. Collect and remove clippings. Do not use chemical lawn treatments. Occasionally leave off cutting for a few weeks for a 'flowery hiccup' for show and to set seed.	Areas at the front of the church, around tended graves and in a network of paths. Areas with interesting and attractive low-growing plants, e.g. mouse-eared hawkweed, hoary plaintain. Areas of very high fertility that are not desired to turn into rank grass.
Spring meadows No cut until early summer and then cut to 80 mm every three weeks until the autumn. The first cut should be after the main flowers have shed their seed. This will vary according to whether the season is forward or late and on the flowering periods of the main plants (look up in flower book). Mid-June to mid-July is often right. The main cut MUST be removed.	Areas where the first cut is already quite late to show off spring flowers, e.g. daffodils, cowslips. Areas of low fertility with early flowering plant species. Areas at an intermediate distance from the church.

UNSUITABLE FOR	NOTES
Soils of low fertility that can be left to grow longer. Areas with interesting butterflies and grasshoppers.	For fertile soils it may be possible to reduce their fertility over several years by raking occasionally and faithfully removing cuttings. Short grass and bare ground is good for soil burrowing insects, e.g. bumble-bees.
Very fertile soils. Where there is plentiful cow parsley (cow parsley can be checked by a cut in April set high). Where there are many butterflies and grasshoppers.	Many churchyards have a preponderance of spring flowers that do well in this regime, perhaps because it is common to leave the first cut to May in some areas. A very wet season may require an early cut before the grass is unmanageable. When establishing a spring meadow, the first cut should be delayed by only two weeks each year, carefully watching for any ill effects of delay, until the desired cutting date is achieved.

GRASS CUTTING	SUITABLE FOR
Summer meadows	
Cut at 80 mm every three weeks until about the end of May, then cease cutting until late August.	Areas of low fertility or during very dry summers.
Take the main cut and then resume frequent mowing until October.	Areas with late flowering plants, e.g. ox-eye daisy, field scabious.
The last cut before the summer break could be at a higher setting.	Areas at an intermediate distance from the church.
The break could coincide with the onset of drought.	
The exact timing will depend on weather and species present.	
The main cut MUST be removed.	
Long grass: annual cut	
The grass is left long and only cut once or twice a year.	Areas that are already left long.
The cut should be in either July or October or both.	Areas of low fertility where the 'Spring Meadow' regime is being gradually lengthened.
Two cuts are needed for fertile soils, with sometimes a third cut in August.	Areas at the base of hedges and walls and in shade.
The cuts MUST be removed.	Areas rarely visited.
	Good for butterflies.
Long grass: rotation	
The area is divided into three to five sections.	Areas with many overwintering insects.
A different section is cut each year, the other sections left untouched.	Very low fertility soils.
The cut section will be cut once or twice in July and October.	Areas that have largely been abandoned but are not wanted to turn into scrub.
Each section should be over 20 m in diameter.	Good for butterflies.

UNSUITABLE FOR	NOTES
Fertile soils with e.g. hogweed.	The length of the break should be increased by only two weeks each year, carefully watching for any ill effects. A short break is equivalent to a 'flowery hiccup'.
Areas with many low-growing plants. Areas with many headstones and kerbs which may not be seen by machine operators. Parishes where there is a shortage of labour, or the labour comes regularly spaced rather than as an occasional working party.	Although popularly called 'conservation areas' long grass can damage important plants and is not very good for insects. It is NOT labour saving if done properly: be cautious and take on small areas at first. Weeds may need to be controlled. The timing of the July cut is crucial for insects.
Areas with interesting plants. Areas that should look tidy.	The rotation allows insects to overwinter in the tussocks, matted grass, dead stems and seed heads, then to recolonize the cut area the next year.

Slopes are natural features of diversity in some churchyards. Because of the greater difficulty in mowing them, they have often received a different treatment from the rest of the churchyard in the past. They also experience a different microclimate, with south-facing slopes warming more quickly and north-facing slopes having smaller fluctuations in temperature than the rest of the churchyard. Cold-blooded but high-energy animals like bees will use the south-facing slopes in the summer to get warm and use the north-facing slopes as a place for hibernation in winter. South-facing slopes benefit wildlife most if their turf is kept short.

Damp grassland is often characterized by the distinctive grass, Yorkshire fog, or, if it is wetter, by the stoloniferous grasses, creeping bent and marsh foxtail. Cuckoo flower may be an attractive feature. It may be difficult to get mowing machinery onto the wet ground early in the year. The soil and turf will be damaged if the ground is wet when machinery is used. The grass should not be mown when the soil is soft.

In the *shade* the grass may be left longer between cuts. As woodland plants usually flower in the spring, grass and other plants under trees should not be cut until the summer, if at all.

Weeds (i.e. plants of waste ground) can prove troublesome in longer grassland and they must be controlled to allow the more interesting and unusual plants to thrive. At the first sign of invasion, it may be best to hand weed the individual plants. If the problem is too great for this, it will be necessary to cut the grass just when the main flower stems of the particular plant species are elongating. For cow parsley this will be about the third week in April. A single cut will probably not be sufficient to control nettle and this will need to be cut four or five times a year, or the area returned to short grass. In a few cases it may be appropriate to consider chemical herbicides, but generally they can cause more problems than they solve. Spot treatment is the safest way to administer them, but there is always a risk of the chemicals affecting something precious nearby. Japanese knotweed is however an example where chemical treatment (probably by Glyphosate) is essential as cutting the plant encourages colonies to spread and digging them up only spreads contaminated soil.

The *labour* available for managing a churchyard varies greatly. Most rural churches rely on regular volunteers to do the work of cutting the grass, but there are many other experiences. In some places it is still the custom for a local farmer to come in and take the hay crop. Elsewhere a pattern of working party days has become established, while in other places contractors are paid for by the local council or the PCC to keep to a contract specification. Even a small churchyard is hard work to look after; a large one frequently feels a burden. As some congregations age and shrink they have fewer active volunteers and less money to pay for the alternative. The fashion for allowing grass to grow long probably owes as much to this issue as to a desire for wildlife conservation. The two are easily confused, as when complaints are made about long grass, which is felt to signify a lack of presumed care. However, involving people in churchyard work may be one effective way of increasing involvement in the church generally. Parishes must fully take into account what is actually possible in any particular church. In a few cases it may be possible to interest a local conservation group to undertake initial or regular work in a churchyard. More often the care of the churchyard can become a joint project involving many groups in a village such as the parish council, an amenity society or natural history group, the youth organizations and the PCC. PCCs should accumulate their churchyard fees, supplemented by donations, to build a capital fund, the interest from which can help pay for management work.

Areas full of grave-kerbs and other stones require a lot of work if they are cut regularly. Often they are abandoned for that reason or ineffectively and sporadically blitzed. In such cases there is often the hope that designating these as conservation areas absolves the parish from doing anything more about them. Such abandonment may be inevitable from a practical point of view, but it should not be dressed up as conservation as it gives conservation a bad name. It takes a great deal of persistent labour to bring these areas full of monuments back to neat grassland. The occasional blitz will prevent the area turning into scrub but will also kill many insects and perhaps reptiles. If long grass is to be treated in this way, it should not all be cut at once. Smaller areas should be cut to begin with and a final refuge of long grass should always be left. Sometimes it may be appropriate to allow the area to turn into scrub and eventually into secondary woodland, but the lichens should be surveyed and the inscriptions should be recorded first.

MACHINERY

Cylinder mowers give the smartest cut to a short level lawn.

Rotary mowers are more flexible and have been the normal choice for a churchyard. It is worth getting one with an engine of 3.5 hp or more. There are mowers available of narrow width specially for cutting between headstones. Machines with a disc with projecting blades cope with longer grass and mash the grass less than those with a single cutter-bar.

Brushcutters are useful for areas of long grass. Forget the garden 'strimmer' and go for the top of the domestic range or the bottom of the industrial range. Never use a circular metal saw blade in a churchyard; opt instead for a head with two or four nylon lines. Brushcutters are potentially dangerous tools and full safety precautions should be taken, including face-visors, earmuffs and stout footwear. It is also very important to practise so that graves, trees and other things to be left are not damaged by the cutter. Brushcutters and rotary mowers both mash the grass up a good deal. This kills any insects or other animals that were on the cut grass or even resting on the ground or uncut grass below. The mashed grass is also hard to rake up.

Sickle-bar mowers have reciprocating blades that leave the grass intact, saving most of the insects and making the grass easier to rake. Wheeled versions of these are heavy and not suitable for areas with headstones or other obstructions. Shoulder-supported models have become available, which are reported to be very useful.

The *long-handled scythe or short sickle* are worth considering. If the worker is experienced or trained these tools can do the job of the petrol machines almost as quickly and with little extra effort, but with much less noise and smell.

The *hay rake* is still the best tool for gathering the long grass once it is cut. Modern versions with metal heads are more robust than all-wood models.

Vacuum grass and leaf collectors are available and will cope with dry cuttings. They are damaging to insects because they remove animals from the turf beneath. Where the principal interest is in the plants and if they are only used on part of the area, vacuums are better than leaving the cuttings behind.

Sit-on mowers can speed up grasscutting, leaving more time for other work – and can entice volunteers who may enjoy the ride. However, they tempt people not to pick up the cuttings, and to cut all the accessible grass too frequently and the inaccessible not frequently enough.

Conserving animals

The high level of calcium in most churchyard soils means that they are particularly good habitats for woodlice and snails, including many small species that are often overlooked. These animals in turn can provide food for exciting species like glow-worms. (One exceptionally rare glow-worm was last found in a churchyard in Sussex.) Many of these need the long grass and the mat of old vegetation at its foot for food and shelter.

The timing of major cuts is crucial to insects. The autumn cut is best left to October, when most caterpillars are feeding low down on the plants or are beginning to settle in the tussocky bases. In the summer time, if there are meadow brown butterflies, cutting should be delayed until the females are on the wing and have been mated, and it should occur on a warm, sunny day when the insects can fly readily. A cut in June can almost eliminate butterflies from a site as the food is removed for caterpillars, shelter for pupae, and the adults lose sources of nectar and territory markers, courtship posts and roosting sites. Grasshoppers may be helped by cutting the grass in alternating strips about 1.5 m wide. This way there can always be some grass 10–15 cm high, even just after a cut, while the grass never gets tall. The appearance of these strips can be attractive too, if unusual.

While cutting the grass when it is long, it is important to keep an eye open for animals. Slow-worms in particular are common in churchyards but may not move out of the way of the mower, trying to lie flat in a vain attempt to avoid the danger.

Long grass often provides a home for small mammals that may hardly be noticed by local people. Rabbits and moles, however, can be a nuisance. There is little anyone can do about rabbits, other than recommend mourners to avoid leaving flowers that rabbits seem particularly fond of, such as chrysanthemums and carnations. Moles, likewise, are difficult to eradicate. Deterrents have little effect and professional mole-catchers cannot prevent new animals taking over vacated territory. Where practicable, a new molehill should be pressed back down into the hole; removing the molehill will lead to the surface becoming pock-marked. However, rabbit scrapes and molehills both expose bare soil which can be particularly important for insects and plant seedlings. Rich grassland provides a home for a multitude of insects and so provides a good feeding ground for larger animals such as badgers. If these animals regularly feed in a churchyard, it is important not to exclude them when altering boundary hedges and fences.

GRAZING ANIMALS

Grazing is a good way to conserve grassland, and in some churchyards it may be possible to use sheep to graze the grass. Horses or ponies can also be useful if there is little botanic interest in the area. Tethered goats are useful if scrub is building up. In courageous neighbourhoods even geese may be considered as grazers.

If stock are to be used, the parish will need the advice not only of a farmer, but also of the local wildlife trust which will have experience of using animals to promote conservation of old grassland. Grazing animals can cause offence if people are unprepared for them. Where a family objects, it may be possible to erect a simple portable fence around a grave.

Conserving fungi

Nothing is straightforward in conservation, and different species and groups often require conflicting management. To date there has been little attention paid to fungi in churchyards, but a number of the rare mushroom-type basidiomycetes have been found in Essex churchyards and so presumably grow elsewhere. As with flowering plants, a number of species are restricted to unimproved grassland. Unlike the plants, though, the fungi benefit from the grass not being cut in September and October when they are sending up their fruiting bodies. Wax-cap fungi particularly need short grass through the rest of the year and greatly benefit from having the grass clippings removed at each cut.

Introducing plants

There is popular enthusiasm for developing flower-rich swards. This is rarely appropriate in a churchyard. Any rotavating and reseeding is normally disastrous because of the level of care this requires, which is not usually available. Slot seeding or sowing into the loose soil of molehills may work, but transplants of seedlings grown in soil-based compost are the most successful. Even these need careful tending. However, new species should only be introduced after consultation with the wildlife trust and then should be of local provenance. Wildflower seed mixtures that are readily available often consist of imported seed, which introduces alien genes into local species. Preferably, if plants are to be introduced they should be grown from seed collected from wild plants nearby. The wildlife trust may be able to recommend a local supplier. Some spring plants like primroses and bluebells may transplant relatively easily, but they must not be dug up from the wild. If they are bought from nurseries, they may not be of local stock. There is considerable debate on whether plants should be translocated, but generally, the species diversity of the grassland should be encouraged by the cutting and raking methods set out above.

There is a better case for creating flower-rich grassland in town churches. Here there is less likelihood of a rich sward surviving from the past and so there is less potential confusion over whether the grassland has been specially constructed. In towns too such grassland may have a greater educational and amenity value.

Lawn care

P8   Do not use chemicals.

Lawn treatments are particularly damaging. The herbicides will kill many of the interesting broad-leaved plants and the fertilizer will encourage vigorous grasses that will then require more cutting. Lawn mosses can also be very diverse in churchyard grass and should not be treated in an attempt to kill them. Fungi are also very vulnerable to chemical treatments on grass, including fertilizer, and even trees may be adversely affected.

chapter 4
Stonework habitats

Why stonework is important

Walls mimic rock faces that might be found naturally in cliffs and mountains. Roofs and horizontal stones may be more similar to the edges of streams that may be occasionally inundated. Where there are few natural rocky outcrops and exposures, the stonework of churchyards will be particularly important for wildlife.

Exposed stonework represents only an early stage in the succession to another community such as woodland. In the wild, a fresh rock-fall will expose surfaces for colonization by lichens and mosses. In the second stage small herbs will gain a roothold in the widening cracks opened up by chemical and physical weathering. Eventually, by stage three, these cracks are sufficient for larger herbs with woody roots, or even seedling trees, to become established and these plants cause further breakup of the rockface. The rockface is only maintained by recurrent removal of these plants by further falls or other causes of erosion; without this the rock becomes completely covered with vegetation.

These natural stages of colonization threaten buildings. Human action is necessary to prevent stonework deteriorating beyond stages one and two. Fortunately this also maintains the relatively rare habitat of exposed stonework for wildlife, so long as some plant growth is tolerated. The degree of toleration will differ according to the status of the wall in question. The walls of the church building can tolerate lichens and mosses, while other walls can tolerate larger plants.

P9   **Plants should be tolerated to a degree on stonework. Mosses and lichens are always acceptable, while ferns and soft-rooted herbs should be allowed on the less important walls. Woody plants should be removed.**

Mosses and lichens

The outside of the church and other important walls will gather mosses and lichens on them. No one would consider that lichens should, or even conveniently could, be removed from external stonework and mortar. Some lichen species are almost restricted to churches, e.g. one species in Britain is only known from a church tower in Northumberland. Some 300 species of lichen are known from churchyards in lowland England and about half of these are rare, found in fewer than ten churchyards and similarly rare elsewhere.[1] There may be a distinct zonation of mosses from wall top to base, with different species preferring fresh or old mortar, ledges or slopes. Close to the wall base there may be liverworts growing. All of these groups of small plants support a wealth of minute animal life, ranging from one-celled creatures to mites, millipedes and small insects.

These lower plants are vulnerable during repointing. Limewashing will inevitably kill off any lichens growing on old render. Both these activities can be phased to allow recolonization. Run-off from lead, copper or other metal work will inhibit growth locally, but it also provides an ideal niche for those species of lichens that can tolerate heavy metals but not competition from other species.

Mosses usually pose no threat to a building except when they grow on the roof. The root-like rhizoids of mosses can do no damage, but mosses do absorb and hold moisture. This means that they can keep the surfaces of tiles, etc. damp which can speed up the process of weathering, perhaps delaminating faster if they are very porous. If architects and others believe that moss growth should be kept in check on a particular roof slope, the plants should not be totally removed if any are rare. In lowland counties it is occasionally possible to find mountainous species growing on old roofs. Very rarely some species of lichen can promote the erosion of limestone. If this is feared to be the case, expert advice is needed.

Lichens and mosses are in danger from grass cuttings being sprayed up onto them and from grass that is allowed to grow tall and so to shade them out. A number of species of these lower plants have been added to Schedule 8 of the Countryside and Wildlife Act 1981 and so it is an offence not to have taken reasonable steps to avoid their destruction. This applies, of course, wherever they are found, including on monuments as well as on walls.

Ferns and herbs

Small herbaceous plants and ferns may also colonize mortar joints. Such plants with soft stems and roots cannot break down a wall and should normally be tolerated, except perhaps on the church itself. English Nature has affirmed that none of the plants of this type can break a wall down.[2] Where they are unusual they are worth fostering during any repair or repointing programme.

fig. 4
Ox-eye daisy flourishes within the kerbed grave.

Nearly all wall plants are picturesque, adding beauty and softness to the rugged aspect of the masonry. A number of typical wall plants are escapes from gardens, e.g. ivy-leaved toadflax, snapdragon, wallflower and yellow corydalis, and are particularly showy. The plants of walls are often localized in their patterns of distribution, so that each town or district is likely to have its own distinct set of plants. Churchyards may have some additional species that are not found elsewhere in their area. This has been put down to colonization of the walls by relic species growing in the churchyard. Some native species are almost restricted to walls, such as navelwort, and this is particularly the case with ferns such as wall rue, polypody and rustyback. Another distinctive group of plants is found growing on the wall top and on ledges. All these plants should be allowed to grow, being cut back if the wall starts to become obscured. Similar tolerance should be shown to mason bees and other invertebrates living amongst the mortar joints.

Repointing may be necessary. If so, this should be done using a lime-rich soft mortar, which is best for both the wall and any plants on it. Ideally, the work should proceed in stages so that new work can be colonized from the unrepaired parts before they are themselves worked over. It does take a long time for the mortar to weather sufficiently to permit regrowth, perhaps 50 years or more, so repointing is best done frequently but in small scattered patches. Where possible the plants themselves should be left undisturbed. Also in the case of drystone walls, professional repairs are best undertaken regularly to cause minimum disturbance to the wildlife in the wall. Where a wall can safely be left unrepaired it does provide all sorts of homes for invertebrates.

Ivy can be a problem but it is also of value to wildlife, providing winter food and shelter, and it is the food plant of the holly blue butterfly, alternating with holly. On the other hand it can cause a lot of damage to weak walls. As usual, it is a question of balance; some may need removing, some cutting back and some left to grow. Where ivy is just starting to grow up a wall it is best to prevent it.

The base of the wall is a habitat in itself. It is usually drier, more inaccessible to the mower and is where the wind speed slackens. Often the plants growing at the base are of different species from those in the grass. Pellitory-of-the-wall is an example. It is a good idea to allow these plants to grow, but they do need to be cut back from time to time to discourage woody growth and any woody plants weeded out. The cutting back of the wall base plants needs to be done carefully, so that the perennials are not killed, and in stages to allow recolonization. The space behind these plants and right at the foot of exposed walls provides an important habitat for mosses.

Woody-rooted plants and bracken should be removed as soon as they are spotted, so that there is no chance for damage to the building to occur. Woody plants should not be allowed to establish themselves at the foot of the church walls. There can be a build-up of bird droppings around the base of walls, especially if there are a lot of pigeons, and these can encourage rank growth of, for example, elder and mallow. In these cases the droppings should be periodically cleared away. In other respects, the base of the church walls can be managed in a similar way to other walls.

Monuments

The main wildlife interest in monuments lies in the difference
between stones of different rock types. In general, earlier churchyard
monuments were made of limestones and sandstones, but granite
and marble have been used for more recent ones. Each material
supports different lichens and mosses. The distribution of these
plants is also affected by the aspect of the stones, with differences
between north- and south-facing sides, the degree of slope and the
quantity of bird droppings left on their tops.

fig. 5
A mosaic of
lichens on a
headstone.

The indiscriminate cleaning of monuments should be discouraged
and chemical treatments forbidden. Families keeping a relative's
headstone clean of plants do not cause significant damage. The main
concern occurs when people desire to record the inscriptions on all
the headstones, especially the oldest ones. If the church does not
have a record of the inscriptions, this should be encouraged, but
those who attempt to read them should be very gentle. Rough scrubbing
not only removes the lichens but with them the stone and its
inscription too. Full use should be made of other techniques such
as viewing tubes (which are excellent), torches, mirrors, and wetting
the surface.

There is a temptation with the advent of strimmers to cut the grass
around the base of monuments regularly. This should be resisted.

Like wall bases, the bases of monuments provide a distinctive habitat. There may be localized leaching of minerals such as calcium into the soil. Often the grass has been left longer at the foot of monuments for many years and the plants living there are used to it. One example is lesser calamint, which favours this habitat in Essex and Suffolk. Strimmers and brushcutters can damage the stones too, especially in the case of those stones with a hardened protective surface which, once this is broken off, weather rapidly. Some people spray with herbicide to avoid more time-consuming management. This destroys the specialized plants and their associated animals and leaves an unsightly brown patch; it is also likely to damage the stones themselves through chemical attack.

Kerbed graves are a great nuisance to those operating the lawn-mower, but they can prove a nice feature if they are treated differently from the grass around them. They form a distinctive set of habitats all of their own.

Sometimes the ground within the kerbs is similar to ordinary soil and is home to grassland plants. Because of the labour of cutting within the kerbs, the plants have frequently been relatively left alone for many years and so may contain a wide variety of plants that welcome the chance to grow up and flower. They can be treated as miniflower beds of long grass.

Within other kerbs there may be a layer of chippings up to 30 mm deep, perhaps acidic granite or lime-rich marble or neutral green glass. This environment mimics that of scree and cliff ledges, with drought, low nutrients, intermittent disturbance and low competition from other plants. The stonecrops are particularly suited to this environment, and although most of the species found are garden escapes, they may well have found their way to the grave naturally. The stonecrops are surprisingly tolerant of common herbicides. Another group of plants that does well amongst the chippings is winter annuals, which flower and set seed before the summer drought. Beneath the chippings is usually a layer of concrete that in time cracks up and allows taller plants to invade. Their roots can penetrate the cracks to reach the moist soil below. It may be worth weeding these tougher plants out to allow the smaller gravel-adapted plants to survive and to slow down the break-up of the concrete. Reptiles like slow-worms and lizards enjoy these graves as the dry chippings quickly heat up to give the animals warmth.

Moving headstones is much less popular now than it was. It disturbs any lichen growth on the headstones by changing the aspect and slope of the surfaces. To move monuments purely to make it easier to mow the grass is an act of vandalism. Sometimes monuments do need to be moved for other reasons, perhaps to clear a space for a church extension. In these cases the monuments involved should first be surveyed by a competent botanist who can also advise on their resiting. It is not a good idea to re-erect them around the churchyard wall as the lack of light kills the lichens on the concealed surfaces. It also disturbs those left on the light side as they now experience a different orientation, which may be sufficient to kill them too. A further problem is that brambles and other undesirable plants can grow up between the stones and the walls where they cannot easily be managed.

Stones that have been laid flat in the grass in the past provide another specialized habitat. They can collect standing water and this provides distinctive niches for mosses. Many invertebrates make good use of the habitat underneath flat stones.

Large monuments can be a joy or a pain. Their flat surfaces and sheltered hollows provide further habitats for small plants and animals. But they have often been neglected and in time will be pushed apart by woody growth. They are very expensive to repair and so every effort should be made to keep them clear of damaging plants. Possible exceptions are railed areas. These are very difficult to manage as one has to climb in over some rusty and vicious railings. Often they are full of brambles and it may be right to let the briar patch remain, just keeping it trimmed at the railing. Even in these cases saplings should not be allowed. If trees have been allowed to grow in the past, they will need persistent cutting back, and perhaps the application of herbicide directly to the stump, if they are to be eliminated eventually. Sometimes this has been left too late and the tree and the monument have become so intermingled that the tree cannot be removed without destroying the monument. In these cases it may be justified to keep the tree.

Ivy can damage monuments by promoting chemical erosion of the stone beneath. It should not be allowed to encroach in the first place, but where it has become established it should be removed. It should not be pulled off as its roots would also damage the stone. Cut it at the base and allow it to die back rather than pulling it off, which will damage the stone further. Where it is rooting within the monument it may have to be sprayed

Areas packed with monuments are one of the biggest headaches for a churchyard manager. There is no room to take the mower in and using shears or strimmers is laborious work. There are three options, none ideal. One is to make the frequent effort to cut the area and make it look like a council cemetery. Another is to treat the area like long grass and have a cutting rotation, but the monuments get hidden in the undergrowth and make life difficult and damage tools. This strategy also attracts litter and vandalism in many districts. Lastly, the area can be ignored as much as possible and allowed to tumble down to scrub. It may be necessary to go in and clear it every ten years to prevent it turning into woodland. This last strategy speaks of neglect to most people.

Churchyard geology

Churchyards offer an unparalleled collection of rocks. The church building materials, the stones in the various walls and the selection of monumental stones all contribute to this variety. In churchyards one can study and compare a range of rock types, the minerals and fossils they contain and the processes of weathering. In a few cases there may be exposures of the country rock beneath the soil or even some erratic boulders, but mostly the stones will have been brought to the site by human agency. Some of these stones may have come from quarries relatively close by and so shed light on the geology of the local area. Others will have come from further away, even from other parts of the world, and these tell not only of geology but of human enterprise, transport and fashion.

Monumental stones were erected to be lasting memorials, but rocks, even granite, weather away. This is part of their interest and their charm, but the process should not be hastened by careless practices. Proper care should be taken not to scrape stones with grass-cutting tools, particularly strimmers. As has been mentioned, herbicides can damage the stonework as well as the plants, and stones should not be vigorously cleaned.

The geology of the churchyard makes a fascinating addition to any guidebook that is published on the church and will provide an excellent resource for schools.

chapter 5
Wanted and unwanted wildlife

Insects

The church building is home to a surprising number of invertebrates, mainly insects. Some of these are common to other buildings, e.g. silverfish, and cause no problems. Some are of more concern, either because they are declining nationally or else because they pose a threat to the building.

Little is known about the smaller invertebrates, but most people who clean churches will have come across overwintering insects in the building. These may be a clutch of ladybirds huddled together, or a small tortoiseshell butterfly that is awoken by the warmth of a winter Sunday service and flutters vainly by a window. More securely hidden are bee-like insects, the hymenopterans. This order includes the well-known honey bee and common wasp, and also decreasingly common insects such as bumble-bees. These hymenopterans quite often hibernate and nest in old walls. In winter there should be no call to disturb them, though the increasing warmth of churches endangers insects by stimulating them to premature activity before they have a chance of feeding in the spring. In summer, wall-dwelling bees and solitary wasps may be felt to be a threat to the church's congregation but they are not nearly as aggressive as their more common relatives. If it is felt that some action should be taken against them, the entrance to the insects' nest should be blocked up over winter. (Unlike honey bees the nests are abandoned each autumn.) A more likely threat to these animals is from repointing or other wall repairs, which ideally should be done in spring, after emergence from hibernation, but before the nests are established. The populations of these insects are declining and this is probably due primarily to a loss of suitable nest sites; church and churchyard walls that have slightly crumbly mortar are a key resource.

Other insects are less welcome in the building, particularly those that live in dead wood: the death-watch and the furniture beetles.

Much though some people might desire it, these two species of insects are far from extinction! English Heritage currently advocates the control of wood beetles through keeping timbers dry and ventilated rather than through blanket chemical treatments, though localized applications of chemicals may be necessary. The place for wood-boring insects is not in the church but in the churchyard, in old timber that can be left standing or at least left to lie.

Moths and beetles that eat fabrics can cause much damage before they are discovered in old cupboards and carpets. Dust needs to be regularly vacuumed in these places and moth repellent used for important items like vestments.

Feral pigeons

These are the main species of bird pests for churches, and steps must be taken to exclude them from the inside of the building. They can be discouraged from using the church as a roosting site by a number of contraptions, not all of which are consistent with the high aesthetic standard set by the architecture of the building itself. Roofs, ledges and rainwater goods can be protected by netting, or their surfaces covered with spikes or with tensioned wires or painted with a gel, or fitted with roll bars. Some of the best measures lie in changing the building design, if this is permitted, so that suitable ledges, which mimic the rock ledges of cliffs where pigeons evolved, are eliminated or their surfaces made too smooth and steep for the birds to gain a purchase. New buildings in areas where birds may be a nuisance should be designed with this in mind.

Some may attempt to kill the birds (though many people may object to this) with stupefying baits or airguns. Wood pigeons, feral pigeons and collared doves and also starlings are Schedule Two birds under the Wildlife and Countryside Act 1981 and so may be killed by an authorized person, i.e. the landowner, occupier or agent. However, in addition to moral objections, killing birds is often only a short-term solution and, if the conditions remain suitable, the population will become re-established.

Where a serious problem has developed, professional advice and operators are worth obtaining and using.

Protected birds

The church may also provide a home for less common birds that deserve protection. Most obvious are the swifts, martins and swallows who reputedly have found God's house a suitable dwelling since Old Testament times. Of course these birds can leave messes which need clearing up, but their numbers are rapidly declining and it only adds to their problems to exclude them completely from the church. They are vulnerable to similar activities to those that affect bats, and also to the replacement of gutters. Special nest boxes are available from Operation Swift.

Barn owls are another declining species, perhaps from a loss of suitable nest sites as more and more farms are tidied up and old barns pulled down or converted. Church towers and roofs can provide a refuge for these and other owls and falcons. These birds are protected by the Countryside Act as Schedule One species and they must not be killed or be disturbed, neither may their nests be destroyed or access blocked during the breeding season. A congregation which has them should be proud of their responsibility to protect these rare and splendid birds.

Woodpeckers can be a nuisance to timber-clad spires, especially where cedar rather than oak shingles have been used. In these cases it may be necessary to treat the wood with insecticide to prevent the establishment of the insects that attract the birds. One parish has constructed a decoy spire out of the old shingles.

Other protected animals may use the church: for example, great crested newts have been found in crypts.

Bats

Bats are fully protected species although some people consider them to be pests inside churches. They can certainly cause severe problems with their droppings and urine. Their numbers in Britain have fallen alarmingly in the last 100 years, with one species recently becoming extinct in this country. Even the commonest, the pipistrelle, has probably declined to about half its previous population size within the last 20 years. One significant cause of decline has been the loss of roosts or the death of bats caused by timber-treatment chemicals or other interference.

The Wildlife and Countryside Act (1981) requires that, if any work is planned that might affect bats or their roosts, English Nature must be consulted and their guidance followed. For this reason, a faculty petition asks if bats are present in a church and if the work proposed might affect them. If this is the case, a letter obtained by the parish from English Nature must accompany the petition. Even if there is no need for a faculty or if there is any uncertainty about the presence of bats and whether proposed work might affect them, English Nature should be consulted.

Are bats present in the church?

Churches are important for bats, and very many country churches have them. Churchyards and nearby pasture and arable lands can provide good foraging for these insectivores, while the buildings themselves serve as valuable roost sites.

To discover whether bats use the church, it is necessary to look for their droppings or urine. When bats are active these provide good indicators, but bats may also use the church for winter hibernation. Their droppings look a bit like mouse droppings in that they are cylindrical, sometimes with ends slightly pointed. They are dark brown in colour, about 3 to 5 mm long, although some species produce larger ones. Bat droppings can be distinguished from mouse droppings by rubbing them between the fingers. Bat droppings are not very slimy and will crumble into tiny fragments of insect skeletons.

Droppings can be found in dark corners and high ledges or in any gaps, between walls and ceilings. In addition to the main body of the church, porches, roof spaces and the tower may well house bats, even if there is no apparent evidence. They may well be using small holes in the wall or roof, or crypts and boiler rooms, which they reach from the outside.

Will building work harm or disturb bats?

Bats, their roosts and access to their roosts are all protected by law, so damage to them must be avoided. Before work is started, there should always be a visual check to make sure that there are no bats present. If a bat is inadvertently caught it should be kept in a lidded cardboard box with ventilation holes and containing a shallow bowl of water until dusk, when it should be released. English Nature should again be contacted immediately.

The potential danger to bats of timber treatment is well known, but there are other activities that may harm them. A checklist is set out in the box below.

It is the responsibility of the parish, guided by its professional architectural advisers, to ensure that advice from English Nature is sought and followed. Diocesan Advisory Committees have an important role in examining proposed work of this nature and alerting parishes, chancellors and archdeacons when the work could disturb bats.

D4   Diocesan Advisory Committees should mark certificates with a standard warning in cases where they consider work may affect bats.

Work that may affect bats

Blocking access or entombing bats

Bats can use gaps as small as 8 mm wide (including those in underground and outdoor structures)

- fitting a porch door to keep out birds or vandals;
- fitting wire mesh to the louvres in a tower to keep out birds (if mesh is installed the size should be over 30 mm, with plastic-coated wire);
- replacing doors with more tightly fitting ones;
- repairing broken windows;
- re-tiling, repointing and repairing cracks in walls and roofs;
- fitting insulation too close to the eaves or filling a roost space.

Disturbances

(Just two disturbances over a winter may kill a bat)

- work to roof areas, crypts and boiler rooms;
- moving pictures and fabrics, e.g. during redecoration;
- surgery and felling of trees;
- floodlighting may disturb feeding bats, especially brown long-eared bats;
- work at the wrong time of year. The best times are: winter for timber treatment, early spring or late summer for roof repairs, and summer for repointing;
- changes in temperature regime or draught pattern, e.g. installing a boiler.

Application of chemicals

- timber-treatment chemicals and their solvents, though safe treatments are available;
- use of pretreated wood, though tanalized wood is usually safe;
- poisons set down for rodents or insects.

Where bats are causing problems

In problem cases, English Nature may be able to offer practical advice. They can call upon the help of local volunteer bat workers to visit the churches and discuss bat issues and their possible solutions. They may suggest that different chemicals are used or that specially constructed access routes are left. They will advise on the best time of year to start particular types of work. Diocesan Advisory Committees and their ecological advisers should also be involved at an early stage.

There is no evidence that bats in Britain have been involved in transmitting diseases to humans. Where animal droppings of any kind have accumulated to considerable depth over many years, for instance in towers and confined roof spaces, breathing protection is advisable when removing them.

In some churches, for example where there may be a large nursery roost, the droppings do cause annoyance. It obviously makes work to clean them up, a job that sometimes has to be repeated immediately before each service. The nuisance may be somewhat reduced if a dust cloth is spread to protect significant furniture, such as altar-tables, or underneath the areas where bats are most active.

Sometimes evening services are disturbed by bats chattering as they rouse themselves before their evening flight, or even by bats appearing and flying around the church. Usually they can be discouraged if the lights are switched on. Sometimes bats can trigger alarm systems. In such cases paired detectors may be used (a bat, unlike a human, will not set both off).

The most problematic issue is the conservation damage caused by bat urine to fabrics, wood and metal surfaces, stonework, and especially wallpaintings. The urine is caustic, not acidic, and can etch and stain surfaces. Where possible, important furnishings could be moved to less affected places in the church or covered between services, perhaps with a cloth. The use of wax polishes or lacquer on woodwork, metalwork or floors is often recommended but may well not be advisable for the damage they do to the artefact. The advice of the Diocesan Advisory Committee and, where appropriate, English Heritage, should always be sought before any specific method of protection or cleaning is undertaken. The leaflet *Bats in Churches* produced by English Heritage is useful (details can be found under the heading 'Publications'). In extreme cases, measures to relocate roosts or even to exclude bats can be taken, but only with the full participation of English Nature.

Rodents

Rats and house mice pose a real danger to the contents of the building, and a health risk as well. Many parishes will be prepared to kill these animals and will set traps or call in the local pest-control officer to lay poisoned bait. Others may wish to capture the animals alive and release them elsewhere. This is the best way to treat wild mice that have come into a church.

It is best to avoid the need to remove mice and rats from the church by attempting to exclude them in the first place. This is normally possible without excluding bats and swifts, which use higher entry points. If it is decided to cover the outlets of downpipes to prevent rats climbing up them to get into the roof, extra care must be taken to keep the pipes clear of leaves and other potential blockages. Any wildlife habitats that may harbour rodents, such as log piles, compost heaps and weedy areas should be kept well away from buildings.

Fungi

Fungi such as dry rot and the various wet rots can severely damage buildings. Chemical treatment will be inevitable in severe cases, as well as the cutting out of infected wood. However, the naturalist and the architect will both agree that it is better to prevent fungal infection by good maintenance rather than to remedy it by powerful chemicals.

chapter 6

Disturbed ground

Usually there is little that is distinctive in the disturbed ground in a churchyard (except for some paths), but these habitats have their part to play in the overall management of wildlife.

Paths

There are a number of different types of path in a typical churchyard. Where grass has been allowed to grow a little, grass paths are particularly important for public relations. A wide (1.5 m) path of frequently mown grass with sharp edges demonstrates that the long grass is not the product of neglect but of policy. In addition, such paths are needed to give access to parts of the churchyard with regularly tended graves or to other popular areas, for example a clump of flowers or the grave of a famous person. Other paths will occur wherever people walk frequently and these may be mown or just kept short by the pressure of people's feet. These well-trampled paths will often provide a distinctive habitat for some species.

Gravel paths are particularly important for winter annuals, especially various members of the crucifer family, or even for scarce plants like the cudweeds or some grasses. In other places they can provide a low grass sward full of unusual plants because of the rapid drainage. Some paths are rich in mosses; one churchyard path in Essex has three rare mosses in it. There is also a distinct gradient from the well-worn centre to the edge under the overhang of grass from the 'lawn'.

There is often pressure to upgrade paths to a hard surface to avoid the risk of mud and of high heels catching between stones. This should be resisted for both botanical and practical reasons. If the path needs attention to remain a working path, adding extra shingle is usually helpful. It may also be worth rolling it. Another strategy is to give it a rake from time to time to prevent the establishment of a grass sward and this may need to be complemented with some weeding-out of grasses. Occasionally it may be appropriate to use a non-persistent weedkiller in rotating patches to keep the ground

fig. 6
A path with
a diversity of
low-growing
plants and
with its
edges kept
cut.

exposed for those species that require it. Any chemical treatments must be applied carefully and according to the manufacturer's instructions, and not where thay might kill tree roots under the path. Where a gravel path contains items of botanical interest it should not be paved over.

Hard paths such as paving, brick and tarmac can have their own interest as plants begin to grow up through them, or even on them. If the tarmac is rather loose it can mimic a gravel surface and so can support rare plants. Substantial repairs of old paths should be left to craftspeople.

Flower beds

Flower beds are primarily decorative features. They should normally be kept weeded and planted with ground cover. Very rarely there may be an unusual plant from elsewhere in the churchyard that has colonized the relatively weed-free flower bed; it can be cultured as a sort of specimen and may recolonize other parts of the churchyard from there.

Flower beds and planted-up graves can be of assistance to wildlife in other ways, for instance in introducing native plants and plants that are particularly beneficial to wildlife. Those with winter berries for birds or flowers that provide nectar and pollen are a resource for insects of all sorts, not just butterflies. There are many wildlife gardening books available which list suggested plants.

The flower beds can also convey messages of a religious kind. One idea is to create a 'Bible garden', using plants that are mentioned in the Scriptures. The plants can be used to provide cut flowers and greenery for floral decorations in the church. In the past branches of shrubs and trees (willow was the traditional favourite) were used to decorate churches, particularly as an English equivalent of palms. It was also common for people to put plants with religious associations on graves and elsewhere in the churchyard, which have then natural-ized. Star of Bethlehem is a common example of this. Some churches wish to build gardens for visually impaired people or for other special groups. This is a welcome idea so long as nothing of conservation value is threatened by new flower beds and other structures. It is important from the start of the planning process to involve representa-tives of the special interest group for whom the garden is being built.

Fresh graves and spoil heaps

A freshly dug grave exposes soil of a poorer quality than a well-dug and manured flower bed. If it is not deliberately grassed over, e.g. by replacing the turfs carefully, or tended by the family as a miniature flower bed, it will be colonized by arable species before being encroached upon by the grass sward.

When a grave is backfilled, not all the soil will fit. Grave diggers have minds of their own as to where they put the surplus, but they might be encouraged to put it somewhere sensible, not smothering anything precious, lying against a tree or burying tree roots that need to be near the surface. Similar supervision needs to be given to those who are making spoil heaps as part of building works. A pile of rubble or a tarpaulin under a heap of sand or cement can quickly kill the more delicate plants beneath.

Bonfires

Churchyards generate a lot of waste, especially grass cuttings and floral tributes with their plastic wrappers. It is tempting to burn this, but this can lead to problems, not least what to do with the ash. Plastic and other rubbish is best put in the dustbin. Plant material should preferably be composted, which is better for wildlife.

If bonfires are made, their siting is crucial. It should not be too near trees, neither should it move around or spread. Old bonfire sites tend to attract garden weed species. If possible the ash should be taken away and perhaps offered to local gardeners. If it has to be accommodated in the churchyard it will need to be carefully sited.

Compost heaps

If grass cuttings and other easily rotted plant material are composted, they create a habitat all of their own. The compost heap will provide a home for fungi and bacteria, fed on by various invertebrates, which are in turn food for toads and slow-worms. The warmth of the compost heap is also useful for sheltering animals like overwintering grass snakes.

However, like the bonfire, the compost heap must also be well sited, and not just for aesthetic reasons. It can be as dangerous to trees as bonfires, if piled up against their base. If it spreads or is neglected, it may attract unwanted nettles, etc. It should not be sited where nutrients could leach out and enter running or standing water. There may also be a problem of what to do with the compost as there may be little need to spread it back onto the churchyard. Local gardeners could take away the compost, just as any hay crops could be given or sold to those with animals. Visually the compost heap should be screened with planted shrubs or a hedge.

Log piles, fences and gates

Log piles are well known for being valuable for wildlife, but they come in different varieties. Two are worth distinguishing. One sort of log pile is tightly packed, perhaps with quite large trunks, in the shade. The result in this case is to encourage decay organisms. They also provide shelter for hedgehogs. The other is a loosely packed pile of smaller twigs and branches in the sun, which can be colonized by bees and other insects that burrow into the ends of the cut branches, especially if they have pithy or hollow stems. If cut wood is to be burnt, it should be done soon, before the wood is colonized by animals. Where possible dead wood should be left standing upright, as this is best for wildlife.

Wooden human artefacts like fences and gates are not distinguished by wildlife from other examples of dead wood unless they have been chemically treated. They will gradually rot away. If fences and such like play host to an interesting variety of lichens, mosses and fungi, they should be treated respectfully. If a fence has been treated, this treatment should be kept up so that colonization by wildlife does not start.

Waste areas

In most churchyards there are areas that have been much disturbed and are now covered by weeds. Where these are very conspicuous, it may be good to clear the site carefully and to plant it up with something else so that the weeds do not return. Elsewhere these sites can have their own value for wildlife, especially insects. Nettles, particularly in the sun and sheltered from the wind, are a good example of this. They attract many insects, from butterflies to ladybird larvae. Nettles need attention however: they should not be allowed to spread and some will need to be cut down in June to encourage new growth for egg-laying butterflies to use. Garlic mustard, though, is best left uncut until the end of July when the orange tip caterpillar leaves to pupate.

Scrub

Where disturbed ground has been neglected for a long time, woody plants can invade such as bramble, elder and sycamore. This is a particular problem where a churchyard has large areas of densely-packed monuments, especially kerbs. Our eyes generally associate such plants with neglect. This incipient secondary woodland is of some value to wildlife, but less so than other long-established churchyard habitats. Scrub should not be allowed to

extend itself. This will mean regular mowing along its border at
least once a year and the weeding out of inappropriate tree seedlings
and suckers.

chapter 7
Trees, hedges and woodland

After the church itself, the trees are likely to be the oldest and most distinctive features in a churchyard. But trees are mortal and they need tending and care. Trees have to be planted, to receive surgery and to be felled, and these actions are sensitive and potentially subject to emotive debate. For these reasons tree care is now subject to the faculty jurisdiction. The chancellor of each diocese will produce guidance on the procedures required.

Trees and shrubs are also important for wildlife. It is obvious that they provide nesting and roosting sites for birds, as well as food in the way of fruit and seeds. They also host many insects. Trees and hedges provide a place of retreat for birds, insects and other animals that may primarily be users of the grassland. As just one example, bumble-bees that will forage for nectar amongst the grassland flowers in the summer, will often hibernate in the ground under trees and hedges over winter where the microclimate will be more even than in open ground. The bark of trees provides another habitat for lichens and mosses too, and the understorey of a wooded area is yet another habitat type.

Planting

P10   Planting new trees is not always environmentally friendly.

Planting may be considered when old trees are felled or when it is foreseen that trees are approaching the end of their life and new ones are desired in their place. In addition to replacement plantings, new trees may be requested for many reasons. Families often want to plant a tree as a memorial to someone who has died. If every burial was to be accompanied by planting a tree, the churchyard would come to look like a forest nursery, shading out the grassland plants of much greater value to nature conservation. The desire to plant a memorial tree may be deflected into the planting of a shrub (as long as the species chosen does not grow too large), not on the grave itself but close to or in a hedge nearby.

fig. 7
The young cedar in the foreground replaces one of an 18th-century pair lost in the 1987 hurricane.

There are often good reasons why planting should be resisted. One is that planting trees can introduce new species or at least new genetic material. This may be alien to what is already present in the church-yard, both biologically and culturally. New types of tree disturb the natural distribution patterns of species and may obscure or obliterate historical features in the pattern of the trees in the churchyard.

Another reason for not planting trees is that churchyards are of greatest botanical interest for their grassland. Shading by trees will eliminate many of the distinctive plants that live in churchyards. Cowslips, for example, will die out under shade. The grass sward in the area of a proposed tree should be checked first to see what of value is already growing there, even if it is visually less significant than a tree. This caution goes against the popular belief that planting a tree is always an environmentally friendly thing to do and may lead to unfair controversy.

Often planting is an unnecessary intervention as trees will propagate themselves by seedlings or suckers. This natural regeneration will be more faithful to the traditional churchyard and will produce healthier specimens. These naturally regenerated saplings will help to maintain the local genetic pool, which may be important for future generations by retaining natural adaptations to local conditions. However, unwanted specimens may need to be weeded out, especially if the young plants start to grow in the wrong place. Some trees like sycamore seed vigorously and can cause a nuisance among graves and so will need to be kept in check. It is also important to consider the landscape design of the churchyard, its history, and its character (see Chapter 8). As the tree grows would it impinge on the church, the boundary wall, a river bank, or the highway; or damage underground archaeology; or get in the way of a future church extension or future burials? Are the soil and climate suitable? Is it a species of tree that can cause problems? Advice on how best to plant trees successfully is given towards the end of the chapter.

The Churchyards Handbook has a checklist before planting a tree (p. 102). The planting of trees generally requires a faculty.

Inspections

Trees can be dangerous both to people and property. In addition to the prudent obligation to look after the church's own property, when a third party is injured or has his or her property damaged by a tree, the owner of the tree is legally liable if indications of the risk evident to an observer have been ignored. A higher standard of care may well be expected of a public body, such as a church, than an individual. The local authority can require a dangerous tree to be felled. Regular inspections will alert a PCC to the possible need for work on trees and this can then be budgeted for.

P11   Trees should be inspected annually.

The inspection need not be carried out by someone with specialist knowledge, so long as the individual has a knowledge 'greater than that of a countryman not practically concerned with tree care'; any causes for concern should be referred to an expert. It is becoming evident that an occasional survey by a professional is advisable. Those who are conducting the formal inspections should consult reference works (the major ones are listed under 'Publications'). However, churchwardens and others as they walk about the churchyard should keep their eyes open. They may notice some of the conditions outlined below. These should alert them to take advice.

The siting of trees may raise questions. New structures may have been erected near them or they may have grown near to existing structures. Archaeological features may have recently been discovered or remembered. Are buildings or walls threatened? Have saplings established themselves on or at the base of walls and monuments and need to be removed? Are overhead cables in danger of being touched? (In this case, the owners of the cable usually have a duty to prune the tree and so should be contacted.) Does the tree shape need to be maintained by pruning or pollarding?

Perhaps it is noticed that the trees do not look fully healthy:

Leaves: are they small, sparse, pale or deformed? Do they flush late or drop early? Is part or all of the tree affected? 'Stag-headed' trees, especially oak and ash, are usually still healthy despite their appearance. Ivy, which is so valuable for wildlife, is not a threat to healthy trees unless it has grown extensively into the crown where it may catch the wind or, in extreme cases, cover the host tree's foliage. For aesthetic reasons ivy should be removed from Irish yews and similar trees.

Bark: are there cankers, fungi, scale insects or fluid seepage down the bark? Are there areas of depressed bark? Where bark has been removed, is the callus growing back? Is the bark loose? Has the bark been damaged by strimmers or stripped by animals?

Branches and trunk: are there cavities, particularly between the basal buttresses? Are there pruning wounds with decayed wood, perhaps hidden by a hard surface or paint? Are there weak forks, e.g. Y-shaped, rubbing branches or pollard stumps? Are there dead branches or abrupt bends? Are there wires or other materials tied around the branch or trunk that will kill the branch unless removed? Is there lightning or storm damage?

Roots: look for surface features. Are there fungal bodies (although these may well be of harmless or even beneficial fungi)? Are there soil cracks or domes? Is the tree leaning? Has there been site disturbance?

The symptoms above do not prove that a tree is diseased, let alone dangerous. Many diseased trees withstood the 1987 hurricane while their healthy neighbours fell. However, these symptoms may indicate that expert advice should be obtained. Often the district council can provide this.

Most tree surgery will meet with approval if professionally recommended. More difficult is to decide when the felling of a tree is justified. If there is a danger that the tree might fall suddenly, perhaps if it is leaning severely or the trunk is badly rotted, then there is a clear safety reason for felling it. More often it is better to lop the dangerous branches rather than to fell the whole tree. If the tree is posing a threat to a free-standing wall it may be possible to save the tree by modifying the wall.

That a tree is dead or dying is not sufficient justification on its own for felling it. Where a tree is well away from property and thorough-fares leaving it to die, perhaps topping it first, will provide a whole range of new habitats that are increasingly scarce.

There are some trees that because of their age or other features are so important that they should be retained and treated in almost all circumstances. These might include yew trees that may be older than the church building, perhaps 2,000 years old or more, or other 'champion' trees (i.e. exceptionally large or old for their species).

Tree surgery and felling

Where any surgery or felling is proposed, a check must be made whether the tree concerned is subject to a Tree Preservation Order or lies within a conservation area. In these cases the local authority planning department must be asked for its permission. The definition of a tree for this purpose is one with a diameter over 75 mm. Where trees are next to a watercourse, the National Rivers Authority must be consulted. Almost certainly a faculty will be needed for tree surgery or felling.

The church architect should be consulted if it is proposed to fell a tree near a building. Just as a tree too close to the walls may absorb water from a clay soil and cause subsidence, conversely, if it is felled, the clay will gradually swell again which may cause problems.

It is appropriate for parishes to undertake the routine maintenance of trees themselves. This would include formative pruning (pruning small branches to encourage a good shape), crown lifting for access (cutting back small low branches where it is necessary to walk underneath) and removing split, broken or dead branches where these are under 50 mm in diameter and easily accessible.

More substantial work can be dangerous and should only be undertaken by trained people who are fully insured, with personal accident and public liability up to very substantial sums. It is sensible to use firms approved by the Arboricultural Association, or Certified Arborists of the International Society of Arboriculture, or recommended by the local authority. The proposed works should be fully described in a specification and method statement accompanying the faculty petition and should be carried out to British Standard BS3998 'Recommendations for Tree Work'.

Coppicing is not the same as felling. When a tree is coppiced, it is cut down close to ground level but in the expectation that it will send up new shoots. This can be undertaken every ten to twenty years almost indefinitely, the tree becoming an aged bowl with a ring of young stems growing strongly from it. Coppicing is a necessary procedure to sustain the life and purpose of some trees, and is especially recommended for hazel. A coppiced hedge will not perform its function if it grows too high. In the case of elms, where these have apparently died through Dutch elm disease, suckers often remain uninfected until they reach about 5 m, when they become sufficiently large to become infected. Thus regularly coppicing elm may preserve the tree for the future.

Pollarding is another traditional way of managing trees, especially for avenues of lime. This involves topping the tree at pollard height, perhaps 3 m, and then periodically cutting off the branches that grow from this point. Pollarded trees need to be maintained as such. If this is neglected, the branches can grow so large that they pull the boss apart. Where pollarding has been neglected, advice from those experienced in veteran tree care is essential.

Thinning a group of trees may cause consternation locally. However, it is often wise to plant more trees than are intended to grow to maturity and then to fell the surplus in due course to achieve the right distance between the remaining trees.

The wood and timber produced by tree work may be of financial value to the PCC. Unfortunately, because of the difficulty in getting lifting equipment into and across a churchyard safely, the wood usually has to be cut up *in situ* and may only be suitable as fire-wood; this may not recoup the cost of logging it. Some woods are highly prized for cabinet work, particularly yew, box, walnut and pear, and these may be sold to local crafts-people and hobbyists. If there is room, there is considerable wildlife value in leaving cut wood in stacks, some open, some dense, in the shade where possible.

Tree stumps are usually difficult to remove. Again there is wildlife value in leaving stumps to rot away gradually. It may be appropriate for the mower to leave a patch of longer grass around the stump. If the stump does need to be removed it can be done by using a stump-grinding machine, pulling them (so long as a good length of trunk is still attached), burning or just digging them up. Explosives are not recommended.

Some trees, especially pollarded ones, produce a lot of shoots at the base of the tree. These usually need to be cut back regularly, but as they can be of benefit to wildlife, particularly as a corridor for small mammals, they are best cut in a rotation of, say, three years.

Trees and building construction

Plans for a new building or extension should include consideration of how it will fit in with existing trees. The new buildings should not come too near trees of importance, and as few trees as possible should be felled.

The design for the surroundings should not include altering the soil level around a tree or cutting its roots. The area above a tree's roots should not be fully paved in such a way that it cannot receive rainwater.

During construction it is important not to damage trees that are to be kept and it is wise to fence them off. Bright placards can also be hung from them to remind contractors to take care. Particular hazards include knocks causing bark damage, soil being compacted or disturbed, building materials being stacked on top of roots, and carelessness with chemicals and fire. There is also a danger from leaks and spills from heating fuel tanks.

There is a British Standard BS5837 'Code of Practice for Trees in relation to Construction.'

Hedges

Planting. The siting and choice of species for planting as a hedge need as much planning as for trees intended to be full-grown. A new hedge will sometimes be desired, perhaps around an extension to the churchyard, to conceal a view or to replace a fence. Hedges make good wind breaks and are more effective than walls, which create turbulence. They can also provide valuable security to keep unwanted people and stock out of the churchyard.

A well-maintained hedge of fair width will usually regenerate itself but hedges can become thin and gappy. In these cases, new plants will need to be added or even the whole hedge renewed. As with trees, grants may be available for hedge planting. Ancient hedges (and many boundary hedges of churchyards will be ancient), are typically rich in native species of trees and shrubs and so existing species should be used to fill in the gaps to preserve the archaeological meaning of the hedge. It is argued that it is possible to estimate the age of a hedge by the number of species composing it; if this is true, adding new species will make it appear artificially old. On the other hand, for new or recent hedges, it may be appropriate to plant a large variety of species, as this in itself is typical of our age.

Factors to be taken into account in choosing species for hedges include the desired size, how frequently they will be clipped, the possible need to keep out stock or human trespassers, and the wildlife value. Non-native species are currently out of fashion, though they could be a suitable choice for a new hedge in an urban churchyard. The over popular *Cupressocyparis leylandii* is rarely fitting.

Maintenance. Many hedges will be maintained as regularly clipped garden hedges, but others will be more suitably maintained as country hedges. In these cases there is an additional value for wildlife, though this value decreases if the hedge is neglected and becomes gappy. One scheme is to cut hedges each side on alternate years in an approximately A-shaped profile with vegetation allowed to grow at their bases. There are various devices by which hedges can be of special benefit to birds. A gap of three to four years between cuts can be left. Generally hedges should be cut in late winter to make the most of winter food such as berries. Hedge cutting should certainly avoid the nesting season of April to early July. The hedge height makes a significant difference to the number of bird species that can nest in it. If hedges are over 2 m high they can support over ten species of birds, but this is reduced to only three species if the hedges are shorter. Insects derive advantage where the hedges are scalloped to make a series of sheltered bays and where some sprigs are allowed to project from the hedge line.

Some hedges may need laying (also called plashing) from time to time. Self-propagated tree saplings should be allowed to grow up through the hedge to form the standard trees of the future. A few hedges are maintained by coppicing, i.e. cutting the hedge right down to coppice stool height. This method is particularly valuable to restore thickness in a gappy hedge or where there are many elms. Such a hedge might then be kept as a normal hedge afterwards or allowed to grow straight up to about 4 m before being coppiced again. Other 'hedges' may take the form of a row of stubs (short pollards).

Generally it is undesirable to remove a hedge. If it becomes necessary, a check must be made first that it is not an ancient and historic hedge. This can be estimated from the composition of the tree species and from the study of old documents and maps.

The understorey

The shade cast by trees changes the vegetation, the so-called understorey, that grows beneath them. In churchyards this ranges from mown grassland to something like the understorey of a woodland. Where the shade is not too dense, as under isolated deciduous trees, the grass beneath can be mown with the rest of the churchyard. Often this grass will be composed of different species and include more broad-leaved plants. Because these plants may be less adapted to regular grazing than those of open grassland and because the shade limits their rate of growth, this grass may need less frequent mowing, and may tolerate it less. Where there are evergreen trees and shrubs that have foliage almost to ground level virtually nothing will grow beneath them.

Beneath a substantial group of trees, the ground may be like a woodland floor. This will greatly increase the diversity of species in the churchyard without much increasing the burden of maintenance. It is unnecessary, and indeed detrimental, to mow under this type of shade. There may, in more formal churchyards, be a desire to mow up to and slightly into the shaded area, but if possible the taller vegetation should be allowed to extend out into the sunnier belt along the woodland edge. This will still need the occasional cut to prevent the trees from spreading. Certain plants such as nettles and sycamore saplings should be weeded out if they seem to be dominating, but ivy does not pose a threat to healthy trees and can often be permitted to grow up them. If it is to be removed, it should be cut at the base and allowed to die before being pulled off the tree, to prevent damage to the bark.

On the trees themselves it may be possible to erect bird and bat boxes. The local wildlife trust should be able to advise on where best to put each type.

Planting and aftercare

It is sad that so many planted trees die in their early years: clearly it is best to plant appropriately and well. Gardening and tree care books set out the full details, but there is room to list the common faults and how to avoid them.

- Trees for planting are available from nurseries in a variety of sizes, from one-year-old transplants to semi-mature specimens. The larger trees are more expensive, require more care, and become established more slowly. Unless immediate impact is essential or the site is vulnerable to trampling, *plant small.*

- *Inspect the quality* of the delivered plants. Bare-rooted plants, freshly dug, are the best in many cases, but the roots should be kept in a plastic bag right up to the moment of planting to keep the roots moist.

- *Dig a hole wide enough* for the roots to fit in without any bending or twisting. Should it be necessary to dig deeper than 0.5 m a faculty will be necessary (to prevent damage to archaeology).

- Competition from other plants can severely affect young trees, and mown grass is especially competitive. Maintain a *weed-free area* of one square metre around each newly planted tree until it is established, by hand weeding, spraying, or preferably by mulching with well-rotted manure or a 500-gauge black polythene mat.

- A small specimen, properly planted and well mulched will not normally need watering, except in very dry weather when newly planted trees may begin to wilt and may die if left unwatered. As soon as wilting starts *water sufficiently* to relieve it. Ensure the planting pit will not be prone to waterlogging by constructing drainage if necessary when it is dug.

- If necessary *prune to ensure a single leader* and to reduce water stress, but only prune while the plant is dormant.

- Stakes and ties should only be used for half standards or larger. This is to hold the root ball while new roots grow, not for supporting the tree. The stake should not be more than one-third the height of the tree. Badly fitted stakes and ties, or those left on too long without adjustment, can do more harm than good. *Fit stakes and ties properly, adjust them regularly, remove them when not necessary* (often after 3 years).

- *Tree shelters* are translucent plastic tubes that provide a sheltered environment for early growth and protect from rabbit damage. They should only be used on transplants and whips (trees under 1.2 m high). Tree shelters should remain in place until they become brittle and begin to break up, usually after four or five years, at which time they can be removed.

- If tree shelters are not being used, *plastic spiral guards* are likely to be necessary to prevent rabbit damage. These can be left on the tree until they no longer fit round the stem, but they must be adjusted occasionally to ensure they expand properly.

- *Keep strimmers well away* – they should not be needed around the tree anyway if it is properly weed-free and they will damage the bark, allowing entry of disease that will weaken the tree and may lead to its death.

- In later years attend to *formative pruning* such as pruning out weak forks and selecting a leader, shortening any wide-sweeping laterals, and removing crossing branches and dead shoots. Crown-lift the tree as it grows older to allow access underneath as necessary, or leave the drooping branches to touch the ground, where they may root and prolong the life of the tree. More major work will require permission.

Thoughtfulness for trees

Established and recently planted trees alike are living beings and require care if they are to live and flourish. Here are some ideas on how to be thoughtful for them:

- *Bonfires* near the base of trees can kill more than the leaves above, but also the roots below and the butt of the trunk. Infection can gain entry here and the whole tree may be fatally compromised. Keep bonfires well away.
- *Compost heaps and soil heaps* can encourage rot in the trunk and make it more difficult for the roots to breathe. Keep them away.
- *Burials close to trees* can sever their root system significantly. Where a tree is particularly substantial and beautiful, digging should be avoided within 10 m of the tree.
- The bark of trees can easily be damaged by *strimmers, mowers and cars*. Keep them away.
- *Don't attach things* to trees, e.g. noticeboards, lights, fencing.
- The soil around a tree can be *compacted* by cars and other heavy weights being driven on it, particularly in winter months. This can damage the root system.
- Soil can become contaminated with various *chemicals*, which can harm the tree; road de-icing salt, spilt fuel, and herbicides are the most common.
- *Building work* can cause a lot of damage to trees. Contractors must be required and reminded to work to BS5837 'Code of Practice for Trees in relation to Construction'.
- *Don't surround trees* with concrete, stone or other pavements and structures or lower the ground level.
- *Veteran trees*, both yews and other species, may require special care. Professional advice should be sought before doing anything to them. Keep them free of ivy, elder and bramble.
- Don't let *woody growth*, e.g. saplings and suckers, become established where it will cause problems, e.g. at the base of walls or monuments.
- Some trees, particularly lime, produce large numbers of shoots around their base (*epicormic growth*). If this is near walls or paths the shoots need pruning off every year.

Record keeping

It is good practice to record plantings, fellings and other major tree work in the church logbook with a note of the ring counts of felled trees. The church property register should contain a list of the significant trees, and should be supplemented by a plan of the churchyard and of its trees, together with copies of recent tree inspection reports. Photographs could be taken from time to time, especially if changes are made, such as tree felling.

Ideally a record of all wildlife surveys and management regimes should be kept by the PCC for posterity, of the grass, monuments, and other habitats, as well as of the trees. These records will be useful for scientific research and for future management planning. They will also be a fascinating source for social historians.

The churchyard itself should be seen as the best record of its own history and treasured as such.

fig. 8
Beauty and dignity: a circular patch of wild flowers in Belchamp Otten church-yard.

chapter 8

Landscape design

The history of churchyard design

In many parishes the churchyard will be the site of longest dedicated land use. Burials often pre-date the current building, and there may be remnants of antiquities including earthworks. The site and shape of the churchyard will be related to the patterns of settlement and their history.

The hedges of a churchyard may be of historical importance as markers of ancient boundaries. These boundaries may lie on lines that extend through the parish and relate to features of village settlement. The trees in a churchyard may also indicate earlier phases of the landscape. Even the grassland may be a historic feature if it retains the composition and character that were once typical prior to the eight-eenth century. A richly diverse grass sward should be preserved for history's sake, as well as for nature's. Any new feature, especially a tree, needs to be added to a churchyard with sensitivity to its history.

We know little about the early appearance of churchyards. In the medieval period their economic use as agricultural land for the parson may have been primary and possibly trees were restricted to the boundary hedges. The grass may often have been managed as a hay meadow, with livestock grazing the aftermath (though how this worked alongside the earlier-planted yew trees is hard to know). Parts of churchyards may have been set aside as sacred gardens, as is known from monasteries, perhaps with a maze cut in the grass to be walked meditatively as a miniature pilgrimage. Physic herbs may have been grown, or flowers for decorating the church. Families have probably been planting out on graves for generations, and some of the unexpected native plants in churchyards may have arrived in this way, as have a number of old-fashioned varieties of garden plants that deserve protection. A number of these have religious associations.

From the sixteenth century there is evidence of deliberate landscaping, with the introduction of exotic sycamores in Cornish churchyards.

By the eighteenth century it was a common practice to plant simple arrangements of elms around churches, though most of these have now died. Specimen trees were planted in churchyards, such as cedar of Lebanon, and churchyards might be incorporated into the great landscape designs of the local patron. Topiary was also practised.

The Victorians were greatly interested in landscape design of cemeteries, but this seems to have had little influence in churchyards beyond the introduction of upright cypresses and Irish yews. Late in the nineteenth century there seems to have been a fashion for planting common lime, which was often pollarded, in lines along boundaries and paths.

The twentieth century's influence on churchyards has not contributed to their dignity. Instead of being maintained as distinctive landscapes, as the garden designer and journalist John Claudius Loudon advocated in the nineteenth century, churchyard management has adopted many of the practices of town parks, including flower beds and wide expanses of grass uninterrupted by headstones (the lawn cemetery concept). As churchyards have been taken over by borough councils, many of those in towns have become almost indistinguishable from other municipal parks.

fig. 9
Boundary pollarded limes and other clipped bushes reminiscent of Victorian designs.

Landscape design in churchyards

To bring together the different views on what a churchyard should look like into a coherent whole is the task of landscape design. A good design impels the eyes and feet, the heart and mind to move in appropriate ways: the eyes to a focus and not to a distraction, the feet to a goal such as the church entrance, the mind to truth made concrete, and the heart in awe and joy to God. A bold claim, but study and recall places of beauty; do they not move us in these ways? So begin by letting memory speak and then consider the inherent qualities of the particular churchyard. For the design should be truthful, in that it speaks of the human predicament, the place of nature and our Christian hope. Churchyards should speak of the Resurrection and give encouragement to continue our pilgrimage. Good design incorporates the classic principles of balance and proportion, containing contrasts within a coherent whole. And whatever is designed today is part of a historical trajectory. Our contributions can interpret the past while looking to the future, continuing the story of the churchyard, developing its meaning and character.

Dynamics of architectural space

A churchyard can be considered as a large room or series of rooms, whether open to the sky or roofed by tree canopies. Their walls may be hedges or lines of trees. As we move through these rooms, from the road into the main churchyard, perhaps on to the Garden of Remembrance or on into the church itself, each has its own impact on our experience and leads us on to the next room. It is good to maintain existing compartments in a churchyard, e.g. keeping the hedge between each new intake of land for more burials, even to create new spaces when they have a purpose. The psychology and art of designing such spaces are well known from architecture, but in the churchyard the building blocks are trees and shrubs, whose scale and three-dimensional form are key to their effectiveness.

We are affected by the degree and character of the enclosure of the space. An enclosed space feels safe and relaxing, suitable perhaps for a churchyard corner for meditation, but a commanding prospect is stimulating and exciting. An open plane with a structure obscuring the view instills fear and awe, appropriate before a large cathedral in open precincts. The directionality of the space is created by elements that give orientation. A long, narrow space becomes a corridor; a square invites resting awhile. A church building in the centre of a churchyard will make a static space, while a visual focus such as a memorial set at the end of a churchyard may lead eye and body to it. The slope of the ground will aid or frustrate this sense. The design can enhance this effect with devices like a gradually rising hedge, or rhythmically placed shrubs, or an edged and well-defined path.

Decorating the visual plane

Moving from spatial effects to two-dimensional design, real life pictures usually benefit from framing, a view through the trees or a glimpse of the church through the lych-gate for example. Groundcover may be useful in forming a visual platform for a picture above it, tying together the varied elements in the view. Within the frame, useful techniques include planting a rounded bush beside a building to anchor it to the ground or planting a brightly coloured shrub to provide an accent or visual stop amongst a matrix of more similar elements. Patterns may have a vertical or horizontal emphasis, depending on the growth forms of the plants. Humphrey Repton, the eminent English landscape gardener, advised that, if trees are against the church building, the classical style benefited from rising lines of fastigiate trees while Gothic buildings were better complimented by spreading trees like cedar, oak and chestnut. Single specimen plants are more akin to sculpture and should be placed as such.

When choosing plants as decoration, their colour and texture (e.g. leaf size) are important along with their branching habit. These will often change through the seasons as leaves flush and fall, flowers bloom and fruits ripen. Flowering trees will only be in bloom for a small part of the year and at other times they may be rather ugly plants. If so, they can be placed discreetly among other trees. In a group it is wise to restrict the contrast to just one aspect, e.g. colour or texture, while maintaining a unity in other respects. A wide range of species may be interesting to the plantsman or woman, but generally makes a rather artless impression. Unusually coloured foliage does not fit easily with a churchyard style, but shrubs with light green foliage can brighten the area around an overshadowed church. The effect of beams of sunlight at different times of day should also be included in the design.

Recollecting associations

Scents and sounds can be even more evocative than images, and a churchyard full of birdsong and the calls of bush crickets has a powerful effect. Like the smell of old wood in a church, churchyard odours will remind visitors of gardens or of wild places they have known.

There is a significant contrast between town and country churchyards. Country churchyards usually retain a distinct boundary, but their style should have a certain wild look. Contrariwise in towns, churchyards are designed as havens in a hostile world where ornament and colour contrast with the secular buildings round about. These different concepts are expressed using elements borrowed from other landscapes. In the town these include the municipal park, the domestic garden, and the botanic arboretum, while the country churchyard may look similar to woodland, field or parkland. Insofar as a churchyard already fits these models their use should be continued. So wild native trees will suit a churchyard deep among fields, flowering cherries a new church on a housing estate, and dignified specimen trees with annual bedding plants a city centre churchyard. The style must fit the setting. The details will depend not just on the local history of the particular churchyard, but on regional traditions in churchyard design.

Churchyards inevitably and rightly remind us of death. It is possible to categorize three responses to this key association. In the tidy churchyard the emphasis is on control. Not one dandelion is to raise its head to question the command of humankind over nature. The awkward fact of death's last word is obscured by the rest of nature being put in its place. The overwhelmed churchyard has been abandoned to the forces of chaos, either city vandalism or rural depopulation. Here there is no heart to do more than make brief sorties to bury the dead, who apparently are forgotten as quickly as their monuments are hidden by the rank grass and weeds. In neither of these churchyards is there much visual sense of hope in the Resurrection. For the churchyard in which there is a harmony between human beings and nature, in which human beings are viewed as part of God's creation, there is faith that the natural processes of death are followed by the divine intervention of new life. As room is made for creation, so is room made for the Creator. It is not just for conservation that the wildlife should be cherished in churchyards, it is also how we proclaim our faith.

Ecological truthfulness

Where the model for the churchyard is the dominance of culture over wild nature, authenticity is given by geometry. In a more natural churchyard it is through ecology. Each site has had a complex history and the soil records this history of geology, vegetation change and, latterly, human activity. The soil's distinctiveness, such as depth, acidity, fertility and dampness, should be discreetly emphasized in the planting design, not obscured by a uniformity or an arbitrary pattern. Truthfulness is clarifying the natural patterns and the associations of creatures. This does not mean leaving it all to nature, as if we were not part of nature, but understanding and then using the natural patterns. So, for example, a woodland has a vertical structure of storeys from ground layer to canopy and a horizontal one from central filler species (the big trees and the deep shade-tolerant herbs), through the varied shrubs of the mantle at the edge of the wood, to the surrounding skirt of tall grass and plants associated with hedgerow bottoms. When designing and managing groups of trees in a churchyard, these two sets of patterns can guide what is done, rather than choosing some brash new arrangement. This way too, the animals that cannot be forced to live there will arrive themselves, for it will feel like home.

Designing for rituals of habitation

What distinguishes a human landscape from a wild one is that we inhabit it. The processes of our dwelling are ritualized ones and in a churchyard easily recognized as such. Analysing designs suited to the rituals of habitation in a churchyard should draw together the principles set out so far.

The first ritual is the one of entering the sacred space, traditionally through a lych-gate or through a tunnel-like passage within a tall hedge or through a portal, perhaps composed of a pair of pine trees supported by holly and lower shrubs to the side. The sacred space is defined by the churchyard boundary. Often different stretches of the boundary are highly diverse and so give a sense of disunity to a churchyard. If possible, adjust them without losing ancient walls or trees, to bring more harmony and balance. The boundaries also need to be in proportion to the church and to the space around it. There may be a need for the boundary to act as a windbreak (keep it as thick as possible at low level) or to screen an inappropriate view. There is merit in growing a uniform backdrop to the church's architecture.

The walk up the path to the church echoes the bridal and funeral processions, which themselves mark and reflect life's journey. In many cases the main path is designed already for this journey. This can be enhanced by its having a distinct edge, perhaps a flower bed or a low hedge of clipped box. Along the route, formal, symmetrical and rhythmic features can mark progress. These might be a series of fastigiate trees, clipped yew bastions, or an avenue of larger trees, perhaps meeting overhead. Where there are distinct bends these can be marked as pivot points by planting a small tree surrounded by a few shrubs to redirect the flow of movement. The surface of the main path can be distinctive to emphasize its importance.

The last journey is to the grave, where the mourners benefit from containment, safe but with a prospect to the future. Some densely wooded churchyards may already give a sense of this, particularly if they also enjoy good views. For those who return to meditate, a special area may suffice, securely hedged in on three sides but with a view onto the rest of the churchyard. This is what a Garden of Remembrance ought to be like, a room within a room, not just an arbitrary area for cremated remains. The grave itself is the place of making memorial. The most convenient way is for families to tend it as a flower bed, until time moves on for them. Small shrubs planted instead of headstones create some variety, but too many would cause similar problems to headstones. If people are eager to donate a tree in memory of someone who has died there may well not be room for it, so it should be gently declined. Instead it may be possible to set aside an area for a shrubbery to receive such memorial plants, but use varieties that remain small. Where there is a central memorial to those whose cremated remains are buried nearby, thought should be given at the design stage on planting around it.

The churchyard could be used liturgically much more than it is. There could be open air services where there are natural amphitheatres; if there is no slope, a backdrop with clear grass in front is sufficient. There can also be perambulations around the churchyard, with stations for prayer. Many individual visitors to a churchyard would make use of the same circular path, perhaps even with suggestions in the church guide book on what to see and appropriate prayers. Such an ambulatory needs landscaping to give it both movement and places of stillness, considering the prospect and atmosphere at each place along it. At a more everyday level, those who cut the grass are not mere functionaries and their churchyard shed, however discreetly sited, must not be a dark, untidy hole, but somewhere a flask of tea can be drunk in pleasurable companionship.

Where to plant trees

Planting may be considered when old trees are felled or when it is foreseen that trees are towards the end of their life and a succession is desired. Local authority tree officers routinely specify the replacement of a protected tree if it has to be felled.

New trees may also be desired, perhaps to screen a view, to enhance an extension, or to make a new feature. New specimen trees tend to be planted without sufficient thought, but their visual balance from many directions will be crucial. Trees look best if planted in groups of a prime number. It may be sensible to plant more trees at first in a group to create an immediate effect and then to thin later. Unfortunately such a plan is often forgotten by the time thinning is due. The planting distance will depend on this decision. The planting centres may be regular if a formal look is desired, otherwise no three plants should be in the same line.

It is wise to draw up an overall planting scheme for the whole churchyard. This would set out not only what is already present but what should be planted in future to forward the design concept. Then as families wish to donate trees, or as funds become available in other ways, a coherent planting design can be followed. This planting scheme could be approved by faculty and then future planting in accord with the scheme could go ahead without further diocesan approval.

Conserving old design features

Where there is an old planting design of note, e.g. an avenue or line along the frontage, it should be sustained into the future. This is not easy when trees die at different times causing gaps in the array. One option is to tolerate the gaps until nearly all the trees have gone and then to replant the scheme, although usually by this time the scheme has passed out of mind and there may be little inclination to reconstruct it. Alternatively, as trees die they can be individually replaced, but the new trees do not do well against the competition with the established ones and the appearance is not satisfactory. Two better, but more radical, ideas are either to plant a new row of trees behind the original row or to fell the whole row and replant completely.

When replanting it is good practice not only to choose the original species but even the particular clone that was used. These can vary widely within a species and can have very different visual effects and were often chosen with care in the past. This may be done by taking cuttings from the existing trees.

Choice of species

Design issues

The main question to ask is what function the proposed tree or shrub will have. It may be joining a mass of other plants, e.g. in a boundary strip, in which case it must meld in, sharing many of the characters of the rest of the plants (even if it is to stand out as an accent through one of its features, e.g. flowers). It may be planted as an isolated specimen, in which case it must be distinctive enough to carry this attention. The tree or shrub should have a mature size that can make the desired impact without dwarfing what is round about. Its rate of growth and longevity are factors here too. It is unwise to rely on a single nursery catalogue for reliable statistics on size. The overall form, branching habit, foliage colour and texture of the species or variety all need consideration.

Natives versus exotics

One hotly debated issue is whether to plant only native trees, or to include exotic species. Native trees are cheaper to buy and will fit in with the regional treescapes even if they have a restricted landscape design value. If locally raised plants are used this helps conserve genetic diversity, though this may matter little in urban areas. Conversely, planting the rarer natives may confuse the historical and ecological meaning of their current distribution. Many native species will be colonized by a wider selection of animals, though some exotics can provide new useful habitats such as early nest sites for birds in the case of cypresses.

Exotic trees, on the other hand, have been planted in churchyards for centuries and new specimens will be part of this historical continuity. Whereas natives may seed themselves, most exotics will only be present if they have been deliberately planted and they bring a wide range of distinctive shapes and decorative displays to our

fig. 10
A large, decorative flowering prunus complementing the tended graves in a suburban churchyard.

churchyards. They may tolerate urban conditions better. There is concern that tree cultivars also deserve conservation (particularly old fruit varieties) and a wide range of species has an educational value. In sum, there is no one answer.

Practical issues

Some tree species are associated with particular problems. Poplars, for example, are known to cause problems to buildings unless kept well away. Trees with roots near the surface such as pines and cherries can disturb monuments if grown too close. Suckering species, e.g. blackthorn, create a lot of work, as do those that seed freely like sycamore. Horse chestnuts have very brittle wood and are not a wise choice close to where people walk. Their conkers, and likewise fruit trees, can attract children who may then start to throw them and cause damage. Trees with heavy fruit fall can make paths slippery and can be a nuisance to clean up, while limes and sycamores can drop sticky honeydew from the many aphids they house.

Where a tree has died and is to be replaced, it may be unwise to use the same species since the new tree may succumb to the same disease. This is the case especially with honey fungus and Phytophthora root disease; more resistant species can be selected. Elm planting has been ruled out since the arrival of virulent Dutch elm disease, but resistant plants may become available. The replacement tree may need to be planted a little distance away from the old, particularly if the stump remains as a source of infection.

Clearly there is little point in planting a species that is not suited to the site. The soil may be too wet or the spot may be in a frost hollow. Some sites are inimical to trees of all types. A very windy spot around a building is one example. Other problems include exposure to sea spray, pollution (for instance by road salt), and vandalism. If the soil is very thin, e.g. over chalk or building remains, trees may grow but they will never be safe for lack of anchorage. Ease of maintenance will preclude very competitive shrubs that will have to be continually pruned back if they are not to swamp their neighbours.

Professional advice

In a brief chapter like this it is not possible to do more than outline just some of the issues, and parishes and Diocesan Advisory Committees should turn to professional landscape architects for help. Just as a parish would not think of undertaking major work on the church building without involving an architect, so also it should be equally ready to spend some money on professional advice for the churchyard. There are landscape architects and garden designers who specialize in historic landscapes. The local agricultural college or historic garden, or the Landscape Institute, may be able to suggest names.

Guidelines on how to protect and enhance wildlife in churchyards

These guidelines are designed to help PCCs avoid common problems. Rules of thumb such as these may not be applicable in all situations and there will be circumstances where those who know what they are doing will be able to disregard them.

1. Maintain long established patterns of management.

2. Don't use chemicals (fertilizers, pesticides or herbicides).

3. Remove grass cuttings.

4. Leave small plants and lichens on walls and monuments.

5. Remove woody plants from walls and monuments.

6. Site bonfires and compost heaps well away from trees and good grass.

7. Plant trees for the future, but with caution.

8. Inspect trees annually.

9. Don't dig graves close to trees; keep 10 m clear to be safe.

10. Maintain established pollarding regimes.

11. Seek advice on surveying and caring for the churchyard.

12. Maintain an inventory of the churchyard's wild and cultivated species.

Notes

Chapter 2

1   From the records of Dr R. M. Leaney of the Norfolk Wildlife Trust. For further details of why churchyards are important for different groups of wildlife see Nigel Cooper, 'A Sanctuary for Wildlife', *Biologist 44* (4), 1997, pp. 417–419.

Chapter 3

1   Gilbert, Oliver, *The Ecology of Urban Habitats*, Chapman and Hall, 1989, chapter 13 on cemeteries.

Chapter 4

1   Gilbert, Oliver, *Rooted in Stone*, English Nature, 1992.

2   Gilbert, Oliver, *Rooted in Stone*, English Nature, 1992.

Sources of further advice

The Council for the Care of Churches is the central coordinating body for Diocesan Advisory Committees. It also publishes advice and guidance on all aspects of caring for churches.

The Council for the Care of Churches
Church House
Great Smith Street
London SW1P 3NZ
Tel: 020 7898 1000

The Churches Conservation Trust cares for nearly 300 redundant Anglican churches.

The Churches Conservation Trust
89 Fleet Street
London EC4Y 1DH
Tel: 020 7936 2285

The statutory body for nature conservation in England is **English Nature**. They will need to be contacted particularly where scheduled organisms are involved. They also administer some grants. They have regional and local offices. The head office is:

English Nature
Northminster House
Peterborough PE1 1UA
Tel: 01733 340345

Local wildlife trusts are affiliated to a partnership called the **Royal Society for Nature Conservation** (RSNC) and their office will be able to direct enquiries to the appropriate local trust.

RSNC
The Wildlife Trust Partnership
The Green
Witham Park
Waterside
South Lincoln LN5 7JR
Tel: 01522 544400

For advice on trees, the first place to turn nationally is the **Tree Council**. Most organizations involved in trees are members.

> The Tree Council
> 51 Catherine Place
> London SW1E 6DY
> Tel: 020 7828 9928

Lists of approved arboricultural consultants, who advise, and arboricultural contractors, who do the work, can be obtained from **the Arboricultural Association:**

> The Arboricultural Association
> Ampfield House
> Ampfield
> Romsey
> Hampshire SO51 9PA
> Tel: 01794 368717

Alternatively there is the **International Society of Arboriculture:**

> International Society of Arboriculture
> Troy House Chambers C & D
> Elmgrove Road
> Harrow HA1 2QQ
> Tel: 020 8861 6852

Local councils will have a countryside officer or equivalent, usually in the planning department. They may also have set up local countryside projects with field officers.

If you are wanting advice on the practical side of conservation work, or are even hoping for volunteers to do some of the work, contact the **British Trust for Nature Conservation**. They also publish very useful handbooks on country care.

> British Trust for Conservation Volunteers
> 36A St Mary's Street
> Wallingford
> Oxfordshire OX10 0EU
> Tel: 01491 839766

For advice on pests and their control contact the **British Pest Control Association:**

British Pest Control Association
3 St James' Court
Friar Gate
Derby   DE1 1ZU
Tel: 01332 294288

There are many specialist groups and also more general groups with an interest in churchyards. Please consult your county wildlife trust for details. A selection of these groups is listed below:

Bat Conservation Trust, London Ecology Centre, 45 Shelton Street, London WC2H 9HJ

Butterfly Conservation, PO Box 222, Dedham, Colchester, Essex CO7 6EY

British Lichen Society, c/o Natural History Museum, Cromwell Road, London SW7 5BD

British Trust for Ornithology, The Nunnery, Thetford, Norfolk IP24 2PU

Geologists' Association, Burlington House, Piccadilly, London W1V 9AG

Joint Committee for the Conservation of British Insects, c/o Royal Entomological Society, 41 Queensgate, London SW7 5HU

National Council for the Conservation of Plants and Gardens, c/o RHS, The Pines, Wisley Gardens, Woking, Surrey GU23 6QB

Operation Swift, PO Box 29, Boston, Lincolnshire PE21 0NL

Plantlife, 21 Elizabeth Street, London SW1W 9RP

Royal Society for the Protection of Birds, The Lodge, Sandy, Bedfordshire SG19 2DL

English Heritage, Gardens and Landscape Team, 420 Oxford Street, London W1R 2HD. (Grants for historic gardens may be applied for.)

Landscape Institute, 12 Carlton Terrace, London SW1Y 5AH. (Lists professional landscape architects and managers.)

Institute of Ecology and Environmental Management,
45 Southgate St, Winchester SO23 9EH. (Provides a list of accredited ecologists.)

Publications

There are many and varied leaflets on churchyards, mostly obtainable from your local wildlife trust. Further books are available on identifying plants and animals and more specialist books on surveying and conservation; some of these are mentioned in the notes. Listed below are a few books that will be of wider interest.

Ash, H.J., Bennett, R and Scott, R — *Flowers in the Grass: Creating and Managing Grasslands with Wild Flowers*, English Nature, 1992

Baines, Chris — *How to Make a Wildlife Garden*, 2nd edn, Elm Tree Books, 2001

Biddle, P.G. — *Tree Root Damage to Buildings* (vol.1), Atlantic Books, 1997

Cocke, Thomas (ed.) — *The Churchyards Handbook* (4th edn), Church House Publishing, 2001. This is the indispensable guide to churchyard care, covering legal and aesthetic matters as well as wildlife ones.

Council for the Care of Churches and the Church Commissioners — *Responsible Care for Churchyards*, Church House Publishing, 1993. Leaflet on the legal aspects of churchyard maintenance.

Crofts, A. and Jefferson, R.G. (eds) — *The Lowland Grassland Management Handbook* (2nd edn), English Nature/The Wildlife Trusts, 1999. Definitive loose-leaf manual but written for professionals.

Davis, Caroline, Fay, Neville and Mynors, Charles — *Veteran Trees: A Guide to Risk and Responsibility*, English Nature, 2000

English Heritage — *Bats in Churches*, English Heritage, 1998

English Nature — *God's Acre*. Video promoting care of wildlife in churchyards.

General Synod of the Church of England	Code of Practice *Care of Churches and Ecclesiastical Jurisdiction Measure*, Church House Publishing, 1993. Detailed information on the operation of the faculty system, including elements related to wildlife.
Gilbert, Oliver	*Rooted in Stone: The Natural Flora of Urban Walls*, English Nature, 1992
Greenoak, Francesca	*Wildlife in the Churchyard: The Plants and Animals of God's Acre*, Little, Brown, 1993. Contains excellent illustrations.
Hepper, F. Nigel	*Planting a Bible Garden*, HMSO, 1987
National Trust	*Wildlife in Buildings, Technical Guidance: A Manual for National Trust Buildings Managers, Property Staff and Others*, The National Trust, 2001
Read, Helen	*Veteran Trees: A Guide to Good Management*, English Nature, 2000
Sutherland, William J. and Hill, David (eds)	*Managing Habitats for Conservation*, Cambridge University Press, 1995
Tait, Joyce and Lane, Andrew	*Practical Conservation: Urban Habitats*, Hodder and Stoughton (with Open University and English Nature), 1993. Advice on all types of habitats, including how to assess them, manage them and promote them to the public.

The following three books make an excellent trilogy on tree health and safety:

Lonsdale, David	*Principles of Tree Hazard Assessment and Management*, The Stationery Office for the DETR, 1999
Mattheck, Claus H. and Breloer, Helge	*The Body Language of Trees: A Handbook for Failure Analysis*, HMSO for the Department of the Environment, 1994
Strouts, R.G. and Winter, T.G.	*Diagnosis of Ill-health in Trees*, HMSO for the Department of the Environment, 1994

Index

Page numbers in *italics* refer to illustrations.

and building construction 53–4,
58
burials close to 58
canopies 62
cedars *48*, 61
and chemical treatments on
grass 25
and churchyard design 60–61
coppicing 52
diseased 51
elms 52, 61, 70
felling 6, 47, 51–3, 59
and bats 38
replacement of felled trees 67,
68
flowering prunus 69
grass under 55–6
importance of 3, 47
inspections 49–51
ivy on 50, 56, 58
and landscape design 65
natives versus exotics 68–9
planting new rows 68
replacing individual trees
67–8
leaves 50
lichens on 47
limes 58, 70
pollarded *61*, 61
and monuments 32, 70
next to a watercourse 51
planting 6, 48–9, 67–8
and aftercare 56–8
as a memorial 47
restriction of new planting
47–9
pollarded 50, 52, 53, *61*, 61
problems caused by particular
species 69–70
pruning 50, 57
record-keeping 59
roots 51

routine maintenance of 52
saplings 32, 49, 50, 56, 58
growing through hedges 55
in scrub 46
seedlings 46, 49
in stonework 26
shade under 48, 55–6
shelters 57
siting of 50, 67
'stag-headed' 50
stakes and ties 57
stumps 53
suckers 46, 49, 58, 70
surgery 6, 51–3
thinning groups of 53
in town and country
churchyards 64
understory 55–6
watering 57
weed-free areas around 57
wood and timber produced by
tree work 53
yews 50, 51, 58, 60, 61, 66
trenches 6

vacuum grass and leaf collectors
22
visually impaired people, gardens
for 43

wall rue 28
wallflowers 28
walls
base of 29
and churchyard boundaries 65
drystone 29
ferns and herbs on 28–9
ivy on 29
limewashing 29
mosses and lichens on 26, 27
repair of, dangers to wildlife 6,
34

repointing 27, 29, 34
saplings at the base of 50
survey of 7
toleration of plants on 26
and trees 51, 52
wasps 34
waste disposal 44
weed control
in grassland 20
and long grass 19
under trees 57
see also chemical herbicides
weeds
and bonfire sites 44
in waste areas 45
wet rot 40
wildflower seed sowing 24–5
wildlife
activities that may endanger 6
churches as sanctuaries for 2
conserving 23–4
importance of stonework for 26
maintaining records on 5
protecting 5–6
guidelines on 71
survey of 7–8
Wildlife and Countryside Act
(1981) 35, 36, 37
wildlife trusts 4, 5, 7, 24–5
wood beetles 34–5
wood pigeons 35
wood piles 45
woodlice 23
woodpeckers 36
woody plants 46, 71
on stonework 26, 29
Workers' Educational Association
11

yellow corydalis 28
yew trees 50, 51, 58, 60, 61, 66